ACHIEVING
FINANCIAL
FREEDOM

Be Free of Financial Worries

Bruce Raine

Arbutus Publishing
San Francisco
Seattle
Santa Fe

Achieving Financial Freedom
Copyright ©2017 by Bruce Raine
Printed in the United States of America

The use of the material in the book for educational purposes is strongly
encouraged.

Books by Bruce Raine:

    Achieving Financial Freedom
    Attitude Determines Destiny
    Attitude Determines Your Destiny
    Income Tax Issues for Small Businesses and Self-Employed Individuals

Bruce L Raine
c/o Seattle Arthro, Inc.
111 Deerwood Road, Suite 200
San Ramon, CA 94583

www.BruceRaineTaxes.com
www.BruceRaineSpeaker.com

Library of Congress Cataloging-in-Publication Data
Raine, Bruce, 1949-
Achieving Financial Freedom / Bruce Raine

ISBN: 978-0-9704946-4-1

1. Finances 2. Freedom 3. Investments
1. Title

Published by:

Arbutus Publishing
San Francisco
Seattle
Santa Fe

For additional copies go to www.Amazon.com

TABLE OF CONTENTS

INTRODUCTION

Welcome to *Achieving Financial Freedom*. This book was written for one single purpose, to help you achieve FINANCIAL FREEDOM.

To get the most benefit, you need to APPLY the simple ideas in this book to achieve your own FINANCIAL FREEDOM. Most books of this kind are not read, and the few that are read, are not applied. This is not a novel meant to be read and enjoyed. This is a book of ideas - hopefully life changing ideas – that you can use and you can reap the benefits.

To improve this book and future seminars, I ask you to please do the following:

- use this book to improve your personal finances

- tell the author your personal financial story and how this book affected you

- help a friend who might need this kind of information

I have been blessed with FINANCIAL FREEDOM for most of my life. Luckily, I did not fall into any of the traps that seem to ensnare so many people. My parents grew up during the Great Depression so they really impressed upon me the value of living within my means, saving before buying, not going into debt for any reason other than buying a house and preparing for my own retirement. They taught me that I couldn't depend upon anyone else - not any company or government agency - to provide for me during retirement.

YOU ARE RESPONSIBLE FOR YOUR FINANCIAL SITUATION

Unfortunately, my father did not practice what he taught me. During his lifetime, he spent most of his money on alcohol and never really owned much of anything. I swore that I would not end up like him. I started as a boy working hard, saving money and taking immense pride in every milestone that I reached. I have worked hard at more than one job most of my life and saved part of the income from the first job and everything from the second job. During my life, I have only had one car loan. That loan upset me so much that I got a part-time job and put all the extra money towards paying off the loan in less than one year. I never made that mistake again.

I have made all purchases (both minor and major) in my life using cash. Sometimes, that meant waiting before I could make the purchase. When I waited, it saved me a lot of money in interest costs. Sometimes, I changed my mind during the saving process which prevented me from making purchases that I didn't really want. When I took time to really think about them, I made a different decision than I had made originally.

When I was very young, I planned to retire at age 55. In the community where I grew up, I saw many men work to age 65 and then retire. Many of these men died within the first two years of retirement. They had lost the will to live and without work, they had no reason to get out of bed in the morning. I did not want to suffer that same fate.

Therefore, I made maximum contributions to my deferred income tax programs and invested in real estate. Now that I am retired, I am financially free which means that I have enough money to do the things that I want to do. Personally, I don't want to be rich as the "Burden of Wealth" is more than I want to handle. It takes a special kind of person to handle wealth in a dignified manner.

This book has nothing to do with getting rich. It is about FINANCIAL FREEDOM which simply means that you have enough money to live a comfortable lifestyle and to do the things that you wish to do in your retirement years. If you follow this program, you may be able to retire early. I have clients who are financially independent by age 40. That means that they can retire and do work that they "want to do" instead of work that they "have to do" to pay their bills.

This book can help if you are having trouble managing your personal finances. This book is not for everyone and is not the answer to all financial problems. This is not a get rich quick scheme. But I guarantee that if you follow the recommendations in this book, you will have a better financial position than you did in the past. You will also have a better financial position than most people in the United States today. That means that you will be able to pay your bills every month and avoid getting into debt. It may take you a year or two to clean up the mess of your past but the sooner you get started, the sooner you will make it happen.

If you have trouble paying your bills each month,
Then you can benefit from this book.

If you have credit card debt,
If you have student loans,
If you have a car loan,
If you have a consumer loan of any kind,
Then you can benefit from this book.

If you don't have an emergency fund saved up,
If you don't have anything saved for future purchases,

If you don't have adequate retirement savings,
If you don't have your mortgage paid off,
Then you can benefit from this book.

Does this idea of FINANCIAL FREEDOM sound impossible for you? No way! Anyone who is willing to work, save and invest can achieve it. I have clients who have never earned more than average income in any year of their working lives but who are retired and worth a few million dollars today. It is simple, but not necessarily easy, to achieve.

I hope that this book helps you achieve FINANCIAL FREEDOM.

Sincerely,

Bruce Raine

HOW TO GET THE MOST OUT OF THIS BOOK

This is not a novel so don't read it and then forget it. It is a reference book. Be sure to read the section titled *The Program*. Also, read the chapters that pertain to you and maybe skim the other chapters to see if they contain something helpful.

Look at your personal financial position today. What are your assets and liabilities? What is your cash flow? If you are happy with this picture, then congratulations on the past decisions that you have made. BUT, if you are unhappy with your current position, the only way that your future will be any different is if you make different decisions and take different actions today.

When you get to the program chapters, please see how you can apply these to your life and ACT differently starting today. After all, the decisions that you make today will determine your level of success and happiness in the future.

This is not a how to do book. You will not find lots of techniques and methods on how to do the things necessary for you to achieve your goals. Every single person is unique and therefore will need his or her own plan and program. I encourage you to determine how to make these things happen for you.

As you read, write down the ideas that you get from the book on how to improve your financial position. Start with minor changes that you can live with and then when you have assimilated those changes into your life, make more minor changes.

Take a few small steps towards your goals every day. They don't need to be big giant steps or a lot of little steps, just take some steps towards your goals. You will be surprised how quickly you will reach your goals. If you spent one hour every day pursuing your goals, you would be so far along after one year that you would be thrilled.

Once you have set your goals and started to act, your feeling of being out of control financially with decrease and your level of happiness will increase. Each little step that you take will feel like a small victory and carry you forward to the next step with a feeling of optimism and a belief that you can achieve the next goal.

> *HAPPINESS IS THE PROGRESSIVE*
> *REALIZATION OF A WORTHY GOAL*
>
> *—EARL NIGHTINGALE*

DEDICATION

This book is dedicated to my dear friends, Roberto and Gabriella, in Santa Fe, New Mexico.

The love and understanding that they have given me over the years has been a great support. As my life looked like a roller coaster of highs and lows, their steady, peaceful lifestyle always helped me to get centered and to make better decisions.

My strong desire for personal growth has been guided by Roberto for the past thirty years. This growth has changed me so dramatically that it is hard to describe but I am eternally grateful.

Section One:

FOUNDATION FOR ACHIEVING FINANCIAL FREEDOM

Every great Accomplishment Must be built on a Strong foundation!

Chapter One

DEFINITION OF FINANCIAL FREEDOM

Become financially independent.
Don't do it for the money,
Do it for the person you will become.

—Jim Rohn

What would it mean to you to be financially free?

- Earning $30,000 a year?

- Earning $1,000,000 a year?

- Owning investments worth $100,000?

- Having cash flow of $50,000 annually?

- Owning your own home with no mortgage?

- Having no debts?

Everyone has a different definition of FINANCIAL FREEDOM because everyone is unique. There is no one right answer to the above question. However, there are some basic principles which can get you to your desired position of FINANCIAL FREEDOM. In this book, you will see some of these principles and how to apply them to your life.

> ## EVERYONE HAS A DIFFERENT DEFINITION OF FINANCIAL FREEDOM

I want to keep this book uncomplicated so that you can use it to suit your own personal finances. If you identify an area where you need more help, then you can do some research in that area and prepare a plan specific to your needs. You can enlist the help of a professional Financial Planner or Accountant or Coach. I will be happy to help you if you have questions in any area. See my contact information at the end of the book.

This book is about FINANCIAL FREEDOM and not about becoming rich overnight or anything like that. You might get comfortable enough to have a good life. In this book, I will assume that you will be happy if you can sleep well at night with no financial worries, if you are not concerned about debts and if you are able to retire and live the life that you want. Do you know that over 90% of the people in the United States cannot do what they want because they think that they don't have enough money? This simply is not true for most people. It is not a lack of money that is the problem. It is the lack of management of the money that is the real problem.

There are different levels of FINANCIAL FREEDOM. Each level of FINANCIAL FREEDOM gives you more financial stability and peace of mind.

Level # 1 - FINANCIAL FREEDOM means that you have a job that provides enough income or cash flow that you can pay all your bills every month. This is the first and most crucial step to FINANCIAL FREEDOM which is spending less than you earn each month.

Level # 2 - FINANCIAL FREEDOM means that you do not have any debts except a mortgage. Being free of consumer debt is a major step towards your FINANCIAL FREEDOM. It is a giant step towards eliminating your worries about money and debt.

Level # 3 - FINANCIAL FREEDOM means that you do not have any debts and you own your home outright. To own a home that has no mortgage is incredibly freeing. It is difficult to explain until you have experienced it personally.

Level # 4 – FINANCIAL FREEDOM means that you have no debts, that you own your own home mortgage free and that you have savings and investments which provide enough cash flow that you do not to have to work any more. This could be in retirement or even before you retire.

The level of FINANCIAL FREEDOM that you want is your choice. You must choose every day before every financial transaction. You should ask yourself before every financial transaction:

> **DOES THIS GET ME CLOSER TO MY FINANCIAL GOALS OR DOES IT MOVE ME FURTHER AWAY?**

No matter where you are today you can achieve these various levels of FINANCIAL FREEDOM. Once you start to see the benefits of being financially free, it will become easier and easier to do what is needed to obtain or maintain your freedom.

One way to improve your FINANCIAL FREEDOM is to get a financial advisor to help you make decisions and to hold you accountable for your program. This could be your spouse, friend or a paid financial advisor. It is important that this advisor is financially successful himself. You don't want advice from someone who is not financially successful.

As you can see, how you define FINANCIAL FREEDOM is up to you. This book is meant to help you move towards that freedom. Please invest the time and energy in managing your finances so that you don't become enslaved by consumer debts. Debt is the enemy of your freedom. Debt robs you of your future paychecks because they are spent even before you earn them. Debt will force you into a vicious cycle of working harder to earn enough to pay your monthly bills.

DEBT ROBS YOUR FUTURE PAYCHECKS

People living in the United States of America pride themselves on living in a free country and being free to do whatever they want to do. The good side is that you can achieve anything. The bad side is that YOU are responsible for yourself. If you are rich or if you are in debt, it is because of what decisions YOU have made and what actions you have taken along the way.

I encourage you to take charge of your life and make better financial decisions in the future than you have made in the past.

I encourage you to take action every day that will lead you towards your long-term financial goals.

Your attitude is crucial to your success, so the next chapter will be a discussion of attitude. The amazing thing about attitude is that it is like your financial success in that it depends upon the small decisions that you make each day.

What does FINANCIAL FREEDOM mean to you? Please write your answer in the space below.

_____

_____

_____

_____

_____

_____

_____

_____

_____

_____

_____

_____

_____

_____

_____

_____

_____

_____

_____

_____

_____

_____

Chapter Two

ATTITUDE DETERMINES YOUR DESTINY

Attitude is a choice,
Your attitude is your choice.

In my previous books about attitude, I talked about how important attitude is in every aspect of life. Finances are no different. If you have the right attitude, this process of becoming financially free is fun and exciting. If you don't have the right attitude, then you are unlikely to complete the process and you are more likely to end up in financial bondage.

ATTITUDE IS A CHOICE THAT YOU MAKE WHICH DETERMINES HOW YOU EXPERIENCE LIFE

- If you have a NEGATIVE attitude, you will see the problems in life

- If you have a POSITIVE attitude, you will see the beauty in life

- If you have an ATTITUDE OF GRATITUDE, you
  will experience a wonderful life

Choices are small decisions that you make each day that build to make a better or worse life. Some people believe that you must make this one giant, important choice that will determine your whole future. This simply is not true. Who you are today is a result of all the little choices that you made in the past. Where you will be in the future will be based on all the small choices you make. You make many choices every day and you harvest the consequences. If your choices are taking you to where you want to go, then keep on making those choices. But, if your choices are not taking you to where you want to go, then you must change the choices that you are making. But remember that you are taking many little steps and not just a few giant steps.

To make consistently wise choices you will need a set of values or beliefs that will guide you. You will not be taught these values but will have to acquire and develop them for yourself. Hopefully this book helps you develop those values. I call this set of values your "FINANCIAL PHILOSOPHY".

What are your excuses for not being financially free? Most people have them and use them at various times in life and in diverse ways. Here is an idea that you may not have realized:

YOU WILL EARN OVER $1,000,000 IN YOUR LIFETIME

This sounds like an amazing statement but in today's world most working people will earn over $1,000,000 in their working lifetime. Just think if you start work at age 25 and work until age 65, you will have worked for 40 years. If you earn an average of $25,000 a year or about $12.50 an hour, you will earn over $1,000,000.

40 years x $25,000 = $1,000,000
40 years x 2,000 working hours a year x $12.50 per hour = $1,000,000

OR

Just think if you could average $50,000 a year,
Then you would earn $2,000,000 in your lifetime

OR

Just think if you could average $100,000 a year,
Then you would earn $4,000,000 in your lifetime

So, you are going to be a millionaire, right? Unfortunately, it is not what you EARN but what you SAVE that determines how wealthy you become. If you could live with mom and dad for those 40 years and save all your income, then you would be a millionaire.

But realistically that is not likely to happen. But if you could save some of that money each year and invest it wisely, you could end up being a millionaire when you retire. The earlier in life that you start, the better the outcome.

What is your attitude towards money? My father had great wisdom around money. He taught me and encouraged me to earn and save from the time I was a little boy. My brother and I had little piggy banks and saved our dimes (big money to a kid growing up in the 1950's). We each had a piggy bank and a savings account at the local credit union. There was a great deal of emphasis on EARNING and SAVING. This was a carryover from the Great Depression of the 1930's. My dad taught me about compound interest and saving before making big purchases. He taught me to invest my money in income producing assets.

I had my first business at the age of thirteen when I started a lawn mowing service (this was before landscaping services were common) and I made my first capital purchase: a brand-new Sears lawn mower with a Briggs & Stratton engine. This was a big investment for a 13-year-old boy. In addition, I was a baby sitter and worked part time in a grocery store through high school and college. I also delivered newspapers for many years.

> ### I WAS ALWAYS WORKING A PART TIME JOB, EVEN WHEN I HAD A FULL-TIME JOB.

Freedom is a funny thing. People think that freedom means that you can do anything that you want. But freedom without self-discipline leads to a loss of freedom. For example, you are free to eat what you want, to drink what you want or to take whatever drugs you want. However, if you don't exercise self-discipline, you will become a slave to the very thing that you feel free to use. These are extreme examples of loss of personal freedom.

Luckily, I learned self-discipline at an early age.

> ### THE LAW OF LIBERTY - YOU MUST EXERCISE SELF-DISCIPLINE TO BE FREE

This appears to be a paradox because freedom and self-discipline seem to be opposites. However, no individual could possibly be free without the sacrifice of self-discipline. It makes me sad to see so many people living in the richest country in the world yet buried in a mountain of debt. People living in the United States have so much and yet borrow money to get more. Why?

The Law of Liberty is true with finances also. You are free to spend and buy whatever you want, but without self-discipline you will find yourself in debt and full of worries and experience a loss of freedom. You will become a slave to your debts. However, with the exercise of self-discipline, you will find peace and FINANCIAL FREEDOM.

**THE SCARCITY OF MONEY
IS THE ROOT OF ALL EVIL!**

A person could be making millions of dollars every year but not be experiencing FINANCIAL FREEDOM. Every year many businesses close their doors or go bankrupt. Was it a lack of income? Not usually, it is most often poor management of the money that was received. The same is true of individuals, if you don't manage your finances well, then you will experience a loss of freedom and maybe suffer bankruptcy as a result.

If you believe that you can be financially free then you can do it. It will take time, self-discipline and sacrifice but you can do it. I know because I did it and I have seen many other people who have done it.

But to achieve FINANCIAL FREEDOM you will need:

- a vision of your future life

- goals to achieve that vision

- plans to achieve your goals

- action steps to implement your plans

Chapter Three

PREPARE YOUR LIFE PLAN

If you plan your life,
You will have a richer life.

The first step in becoming financially free is to prepare a Life Plan so that you know where you are going. This may sound very difficult and maybe even impossible. Many people don't want to plan their lives but prefer to just see what life offers them along the way. Life will offer you a lot more if you plan where you are going and what you want to achieve along the way. You don't have to plan every little thing but you do need to plan the important things in your future.

> A LIFE PLAN WILL SHOW YOU WHERE YOU ARE NOW
> A LIFE PLAN WILL SHOW YOU WHERE YOU WANT TO GO
> A LIFE PLAN WILL SHOW YOU HOW TO GET THERE

Your plan can and should be flexible. You are not locked into what you plan. Usually a good plan will have to be revised upwards because you will be achieving more success than you thought you could. When I left high school and went to college, I had no idea where it would lead me. But, I went because that was the smart thing to do and that was part of my Life Plan. I believed that it would give me a better life and it did.

Going to college got me my first job as an officer in the Royal Canadian Navy. But that was not my destiny in life. I learned a great deal from that experience and did some travelling which became my lifetime passion. But, I left after 3 years because I was always seasick when I was on a ship even though I loved the thrill of being at sea.

My college degree also got me my second job as an accountant. I had majored in mathematics which was helpful. It got me in the door but that was all. I had to study and become an accountant. Since I loved it, I studied hard and became one of the top students in my area. This gave me an excellent job as an accountant. But, this was just another step in my Life Plan. I have done a lot of consulting work in the accounting field but always as a sideline to my main career.

My college degree and accounting designation got me into my dream job. I became a Professor and got to move from

Eastern Canada to the San Francisco Bay area where I spent my career. Both were part of my Life Plan.

Teaching was the absolute perfect job for me. I started teaching at St. Mary's College in Halifax, Nova Scotia. But most of my teaching career was at California State University in Hayward, California. I had great bosses, Alan Johnson and Vernon Kam, who guided me through my career in teaching accounting and computers. I look back and I cannot imagine any job that would be more perfect for me. It fit my desire to teach, my love of accounting, my wish not to be strapped to a desk and my longing to interact with and influence young people.

What was my Life Plan, you ask? I didn't have a fixed, detailed Life Plan but one that I amended as time went on. I would review it annually, see where I was at that point and then revise it to where I wanted to go in life. I knew from the age of 5 that I was destined to be a teacher and to live in California. This seems amazing to me and to most people I tell. But, that was my overriding plan for my life. My Life Plan was simple:

- go to college

- become a teacher

- live in California

While you may say that was not much of a plan and you would be right, it gave me direction at key junctions in my journey in life. Obviously, there were not many details in my plan. A Life Plan does not have to be very detailed or complex. It is used to guide you when you are making decisions.

• When I left high school, I was advised not to go to university since I was sure to fail. I almost proved them correct in my first year but ended up finishing my degree in 3 years.

• During my 20's I changed from a shy, quiet kid who knew nothing that I could teach to a confident public speaker who knew accounting really well because I loved it and wanted to know everything I could about it.

• During my first full year of teaching, there was a big blizzard and I remembered that I wanted to move to California. I lived in Halifax, Nova Scotia in Eastern Canada where I grew up. I knew that I wanted to live in California where there was lots of sunshine and the winters were mild. That summer I packed up and moved to San Francisco and worked in the East Bay for the rest of my teaching career.

As you can see these three parts of my Life Plan had considerable influence on my decisions at these 3 key junctures in my life. There were many more times that my Life Plan guided me in making decisions.

A LIFE PLAN IS USED TO GUIDE YOU WHEN YOU ARE MAKING DECISIONS

What is your Life Plan? If I was preparing a Life Plan today, I would look at several areas of life and set goals or plans for each one to live a balanced and successful life. These areas would include those listed below. Please note that they are in no particular order. This may not be the list that you choose to use for your Life Plan. You must determine which are the most and least important to you. But it is important to consider all areas in your Life Plan.

I recommend that you take a few minutes and write down your Life Plan below. You can always revise it later but take fifteen minutes and outline your Life Plan NOW!

Areas of a Life Plan:

- health _____
- financial freedom _____
- recreation _____
- spiritual life _____
- career _____
- family relationships _____
- where to live _____
- retirement _____

RESOURCES:

I do not want to spend a lot of time in this book talking about your Life Plan. I just want to talk about the financial freedom section. For more information on Life Planning, I recommend the book *Lifeplanning* by Robb E. Dalton. As for setting goals, there are many good books available but I personally think that Brian Tracy is the best I have read. His book titled *Goals* is one that I read and study once a year to keep me on track.

I recommend that you read these books. No, I recommend that you devour them and absorb what they will teach you. Be sure to act on what you learn by reading books. Trust me when I say that these books will change your life in a very positive way.

Another important book is *The Alladin Factor* by Jack Canfield and Mark Victor Hansen. This book deals with how to get what you want in life. The authors demonstrate how ASKING is an important method to obtain what you want. Ask is a word in the English language but ASK is an acronym for Ask, Seek and Knock.

> ### *ASK AND YOU SHALL RECEIVE;*
> ### *SEEK AND YOU SHALL FIND;*
> ### *KNOCK AND THE DOOR WILL BE OPEN FOR YOU.*
>
> ### *— MATTHEW 7:7*

If you don't make a Life Plan and you don't ask for what you want, then you won't achieve the success that you want and you won't get what you want in life. Setting a Life Plan and going through the steps of achieving that Life Plan is a form of asking. You are asking life or a higher power to give you the life that you picture.

What you believe about every aspect of life will help to determine the level of success and happiness that you achieve. Next, we will look at your FINANCIAL PHILOSOPHY which will be a key component of your achieving success.

Make A Life Plan

Chapter Four

WHAT IS YOUR FINANCIAL PHILOSOPHY?

If you want to be financially free,
Then you must be the one to do it.

Do you have a FINANCIAL PHILOSOPHY? Yes, of course you do, everyone does. But you may not be aware of it because you never intentionally thought about it. But every time you have earned money or spent money or made a financial decision, you were guided by your FINANCIAL PHILOSOPHY. It may seem irrational or illogical, but your FINANCIAL PHILOSOPHY has been a key part of your life since the time that you first had money.

If you want to find out what your FINANCIAL PHILOSOPHY is, just look back over the past 5 years and determine what your FINANCIAL PHILOSOPHY has been. Ask yourself "WHY DID THIS HAPPEN?" when you look at your purchases, loans, cash balances, investments, credit cards, etc. They reflect your FINANCIAL PHILOSOPHY. This is an important exercise because you need to know how you got to where you are today. If you continue to make the same decisions, you will have the same results in the future.

> ## PAST ⋯→ PRESENT ⋯→ FUTURE

You must know your past and how you got to the present situation. The purpose of looking back is not to be critical and punish yourself, but to learn what you did and to see the consequences. If you are happy with them, then continuing to do the same thing will work well. However, if you are not happy with your present circumstances, then you need to change what you do in the future to get different, and better, results.

Let's look at these 3 points in time in your life:

- 5 years ago
- today
- 5 years in the future

> ## 5 YEARS AGO ⋯→ PRESENT ⋯→ 5 YEARS IN THE FUTURE

If you have no savings or no investments today or if you are in debt, it is because of your FINANCIAL PHILOSOPHY over the past 5 years or more. If you want to have savings and investments in the future so that you can retire, you will have to adopt a different FINANCIAL PHILOSOPHY. That is the only way that you are going to be in a better place 5 years from now.

CHANGE DOESN'T HAPPEN AUTOMATICALLY

Change doesn't happen by itself, you must do it. It takes VISION to see what you want to achieve, SELF-DISCIPLINE to do what must be done and PERSEVERANCE to do the right actions over time and when the going gets tough. If you can see what needs to be done and you are willing to do it day in and day out, then you will achieve the level of FINANCIAL FREEDOM that you desire. It is not difficult to do but it does require consistent effort working towards your goals.

For example, if you want to pay off your credit card debt or car loan, you can see where you are today and you can plan how to pay it off. Maybe an extra $300 a month for 2 years will do the trick. Then you must be diligent in paying that extra $300 every month for those 2 years. You can't go for 3 months and then decide that you want to do something else. Following through on your plan is critical to your success.

When I was younger, I bought a car and had a car loan. I was young and foolish and wanted a fancy IROC Camaro so I went out and bought a used one by using a car loan. But afterwards I was very unhappy with myself because I had taken on consumer debt in the form of a car loan. I decided to pay it off in the next year. I figured how much I would have to earn to pay off the car loan in one year. Then, I went out and got a second job and used all the money I received from that part-time job to pay off the loan. Within the year it was paid off and I have never taken another car loan.

Part of a successful FINANCIAL PHILOSOPHY is quite simple:

> ## I WILL NOT INCUR ANY DEBT
> ## EXCEPT FOR REAL ESTATE

It is important that you determine what your FINANCIAL PHILOSOPHY is in various areas of your finances.

Next is an exercise to determine your FINANCIAL PHILOSOPHY. I encourage you to take this seriously and complete it as best you can. If you don't know the answer, then look at how you handled that type of transaction in the past. It is okay to skip items and go on to the next one.

What is your FINANCIAL PHILOSOPHY? Take a few minutes and write down what your current philosophy is in each of these areas. If you would like some ideas to help you out, refer to Appendix A – Bruce's FINANCIAL PHILOSOPHY. You need to decide what you want to do in the following areas of your personal finances:

- credit cards

- debit cards

- consumer loans (furniture, electronics, vacations, etc.)

- car loans

- student loans

- real estate loans

- savings

- investments

- income

- expenses

- retirement

- giving to church and charity

- making large purchases like car and furniture

- emergency fund

- tax deferred programs

- buying a home

- insurance

Next is the most important part of the book. The next 3 chapters will give you a simple system to achieve FINANCIAL FREEDOM. While it may not seem easy, it is better than the alternative of being FINANCIALLY TRAPPED!

Section Two:

THE PROGRAM

*Follow The
Program Every Day*

Step One

SPEND LESS THAN YOU EARN EVERY MONTH

The LACK of money
Is the root of all evil!

Did you know that most people who are in prison are there for crimes committed to obtain money? It seems that people will do anything for money. Some people will steal, sell drugs or murder while other people will give up 40 years of their life working to gain more money. Some people will borrow to obtain money to buy more stuff that ends up trapping them in a mountain of debt. But it is quite simple to have enough money in your life for whatever you want.

The first and most important part of your FINANCIAL PHILOSOPHY should be one that underlies everything. This rule will be the foundation of all the other rules that you make up for your FINANCIAL PHILOSOPHY.

The absolute simplest way to describe how to be financially free is:

> ## SPEND LESS THAN YOU EARN!

If you get nothing out of this book except this one simple principle and you follow this principle throughout your life, then you will achieve a greater level of FINANCIAL FREEDOM than most of the people living in the United States today. Many people in our society are burdened by debt and they are not experiencing FINANCIAL FREEDOM because they don't follow this one simple rule.

This seems like such a common-sense idea. What could be more straight forward and logical than this? But many people in the United States today ignore this simple truism. Why? People want more. Credit is easy. Virtually anyone can get a credit card and spend like crazy. Making a major purchase like a car or house can be done with little or no money down. You may not realize it but easy credit is more of a curse than a blessing.

> ## SPENDING MORE THAN YOU EARN
> ## LEADS TO DISASTER!

The only time that unlimited spending is a viable strategy is when you have a significant amount of money to start with.

You live on what you earn plus what you can afford to draw down from your savings. This is how rich people and retired people can live but even they must manage their finances carefully. Many people who have started with a lot of money have gone broke because they spent too much money too fast.

However, if you don't have a large amount of money to start with, then you will end up owing a large amount of money sooner than you think. Just look at all the people who run up credit card debt, car loans and other consumer debt that they can't pay back. What we don't see is the stress that they live under for a long time. If they are married, this can lead to marital stress and divorce. In fact, lack of money is one of the leading causes of divorce.

While you certainly can spend more than you earn, you are betting that something is going to change in the future that will allow you to pay off your debts. If you get a raise, that will be the ticket. If your house appreciates in value, then you can pay off the debts. If you win the lottery you will be okay. You are spending tomorrow's income before you have earned it. You are not living in FINANCIAL FREEDOM and this will be a major source of stress in your life.

**WHEN YOU SPEND MORE THAN YOU EARN,
YOU ARE SPENDING TOMORROW'S INCOME**

If you are willing to live a little more frugally today and follow the principles in this book, you will be able to live the life you dream of in the future with complete FINANCIAL FREEDOM. The principles in this book are not difficult to follow or harsh in terms of lifestyle. However, they do require that you live a more modest lifestyle and save money which will mean FINANCIAL FREEDOM in the future which is far more valuable than the "stuff" that you might buy today.

One of the greatest joys in life is to experience PEACE! Peace means that your mind is free from worry. You can relax and enjoy the moment free of worrying about tomorrow, free from worrying about money. One of the main sources of worry for people who live in the United States of America today is lack of money. It seems like a paradox. We live in the richest nation in the history of the world and one of our main worries is about money. We already have more than our parents and grandparents did. While the average American has a lifestyle far better than that of 99% of the people on the planet, many are unhappy because their lifestyle is not as good as some athlete or movie star or rich business person. If you can learn to be happy with what you have, then you will truly achieve peace in life.

> *HAPPY IS BEING SATISFIED WITH WHAT YOU HAVE!*

While there is nothing wrong with wanting a better lifestyle, happiness will only come when you are satisfied with what you have right now. While you may want more in the future, you must be satisfied with what you have right now to be happy. If you are not happy with what you have now but believe that you will be happy when you get the "next thing", then probably you will not be happy when you get that "next thing" because there will always be another "next thing" in your life.

Do you know the Blues Brothers? Their movie is one of my all time favorite movies. What were they like in real life? John Belushi was an incredible comedian and was at the top of his career when he died. He had a movie, a music CD and a television show that were all very successful. How did John deal with his success? Was he happy? Apparently not because he spent his life (time and money) doing drugs which eventually killed him.

His partner, comedian Dan Akroyd, who was achieving the same level of success handled it much better and still is a successful entertainer and businessman today. While Dan may have wanted more and worked to get it, he was satisfied with what he had and didn't need to use drugs to escape.

Spend Less Than You Earn

The average American today spends more than they earn every month and every year. During this prosperous period in our history, bankruptcies are up and financial problems are at an all-time high. Why? The simple reason is the inability of the average person to manage their own personal finances.

Many people laugh at the idea of spending less than you earn even though this seems like such common sense. But how many people live like this today? Anyone who has consumer debt doesn't! Congress doesn't! MC Hammer was making millions when he went bankrupt from spending more than he made. History is full of people (kings and queens, aristocrats, athletes, musicians, movie stars, average working-class families, etc.) who spent more than they earned and ended up broke.

Many people live with lots of consumer debt and no savings. That is a sure recipe for disaster. What happens when you have an emergency? Emergencies will come into everyone's life usually on the average of at least once a decade. Some people who are homeless were simply not prepared for some emergency and couldn't survive it financially.

What happens when the national economy has a slow down and you lose your job? What happens when you get sick and can't work? What happens when your job moves offshore? There are numerous things that could happen to change your financial situation in a minute. If you live on the edge, then when something happens it can push you over the edge.

I worked with the homeless in San Francisco for several years and I met a man named Earl. He had a very sad story. He was an average guy with a family and lived in Hayward, California. He had a decent job where he worked over 20 years. He thought that his life was good. But, he lived paycheck to paycheck with consumer debt and no savings. When his company went broke, everyone lost their jobs and their pensions. A few months later his wife couldn't stand the financial pressure and left him. Of course, no one wins in a divorce so they were both worse off than before which wasn't good.

Earl was on the street because he lost everything and the sudden changes in his fortunes were too much for him to cope with. He lost hope for a better life in the future. When I met him, he was doing nothing more than simply existing until he died!

A simple rule of life should always be:

> **SPEND LESS THAN YOU EARN EVERY MONTH**

Is this hard to do? Not really. If you are always living and spending less than you earn, then you are building up savings and are better able to cope with day to day expenses and then of course, the emergency that inevitably will come along. I know a man named Rodger who decided to live on 50% of his income. He bought a smaller house than he could afford, he drove a used car and he saved a lot of money. What happened to him? He enjoyed travelling throughout his life and didn't wait until retirement to travel. He retired at 55 and is very happy and financially free today.

It really is easy if you just simply decide to do it every month. After a while it becomes so easy that you won't even notice that you are doing it. If you make it into a game, it can be fun. I know a couple who decided that they would use coupons to keep down their living expenses. They have made it into a game. They go to new restaurants often and have lots of fun seeing how good a deal they can get at various stores. I have another client who has shopped at second hand stores for clothing for years. She is always well dressed and has a lot of money saved for her retirement. Plus, she has a lot of fun seeking "treasures" in these stores.

If you spend less than you earn each month, then you won't incur any consumer debt. However, if you already have consumer debt, spending less than you earn will allow you to pay it off with the amount that you earn over and above your expenses each month.

INCREASE YOUR INCOME OR DECREASE YOUR EXPENSES

How do you spend less than you earn? There are three viable answers to this question:

1. increase your income

2. decrease your expenses

3. both (1) and (2) above

It is easy to see that to spend less than you earn you can do one of these three strategies above. Personally, I chose # 3 for my life. It began in my 20's and has continued ever since. For my entire life I have lived by the first recommendation which is to spend less than I earn ALWAYS!

For most of my life, I have worked at a second job to increase my income. I have been doing consulting work for 30 years which has been in addition to my regular job. But I have also chosen to live a more modest lifestyle than I might. I don't need a large house or expensive car. I like to travel and that has been my largest annual expense most of my life. But even there I chose vacations that didn't put my spending over my income.

What can you do to increase your income?

- get a raise

- get a promotion

- change jobs

- become better at your job

- get a second job

- invest in real estate

- invest in mutual funds

- turn your home into a source of income instead of an expense

- start a business on the side

Many people who started working at a part time job just to pay off some debt ended up liking the job or making so much money at it that they ended up quitting their real job and working at the part time one. This is an effective way to "try out" a new job to see if you like it and if you are any good at it. It may seem like a struggle to balance two jobs but many people do it on a regular basis.

The same is true of starting a business. You start a small business just to make some extra income. But soon you find that you like it and it is more profitable than you thought. Maybe then you can quit your job and make a living at something that you love to do.

What can you do to decrease your expenses?

- own a cheaper car

- own or rent a less expensive house

- use public transportation

- reduce your restaurant meals

- buy only what you "need"

- cook meals at home

- wear your clothes longer

- buy used clothes

- take cheaper vacations

- own fewer toys (consider renting them instead of owning them)

- sell high maintenance items (boat, RV, etc.)

These are only a few examples of what you can do. What can you do in your life? Look at how you spend your money and where you can reduce your spending.

Usually housing and transportation are two of the larger expenses in a person's life. What can you do to reduce those? Living in a smaller house whether you rent or own would reduce your costs of housing. Renting out a room or buying a house with a rental unit could help offset the cost of housing. Buying a used car instead of new car or keeping your present car longer instead of buying a new one could make a significant difference. Often it is cheaper to repair a used car than make payments on a new car.

I had a client who graduated from college with no debt whatsoever. She went out and bought an expensive new car with a big loan payment every month. After about six months she felt the burden of making the large payments. Although she loved the car, she decided to return it to the dealer. Although she lost some money, she was happy. Then she went out and purchased a good quality used car for much less money.

To reduce your spending, look at your expenses for the past few months or the last year. Categorize them in some way that makes sense to you. Then, look at each category and see what you could do, or what you would be willing to do, to reduce these expenses. Reducing each expense just a little will make a significant difference. Eliminating some expenses that are not really "necessary" could also make an enormous difference. Once you see how easy it is, you can continue to reduce your expenses until they are less than your income.

What if you "CAN'T" reduce your expenses? Trust me you could if you had to. What if you lost your job and couldn't get another job for awhile. You would be forced to reduce expenses. If you say that you can't reduce expenses then you are only fooling yourself. If you want to you could cut your expenses by 10%, 20% or even 50%. If a rich uncle said that he would give you a million dollars if you cut your expenses by 50% for a year, do you think that you might be able to do it?

The number one thing that you must do is accept responsibility for your expenses. They are under your control even if you feel that they are not. If you exercise self-discipline in your spending, you will see a major change in your finances in a very brief period.

SUCCESS STORY

Here is an extreme example of this philosophy of spending less than you earn. Ryan Broyles is a professional football player in the National Football League (NFL). He earns an average of $600,000 a year. But he lives on just $60,000 a year or $5,000 a month.

Statistics show that approximately fifteen percent of NFL players will file for bankruptcy in their lifetime. This is down from the past because the NFL provides training to help young players better manage their large incomes.

Ryan understands that football is a job that could last ten years or ten minutes. He wants the money that he earns from football to last him a lifetime. His goal is to have his football earnings give him FINANCIAL FREEDOM for the rest of his life.

> ### SPENDING LESS THAN YOU EARN IS
> ### SMART IN ANY INCOME BRACKET

He grew up in Oklahoma where his parents taught him a strong work ethic. He mowed lawns to earn money to go on team basketball trips. In high school, he worked at a grocery store as a bag boy. He was a hard worker and managed his money well but the catalyst for his frugality was an injury to his leg in college. That injury showed him that his career could be short and so he had to manage the money he received wisely to make it last. Part of Ryan's FINANCIAL PHILOSOPHY is:

> ### I WANT THE INVESTMENTS TO PROVIDE
> ### SO I'M FINANCIALLY FREE

Ryan lives with a budget that would make most people cringe but he feels that it is necessary to sacrifice now for long term FINANCIAL FREEDOM. His budget looks something like this. He takes an after-tax amount of $60,000 to live on broken down as shown below:

- 50% on fixed costs like mortgage, automobile and insurance

- 30% on living expenses like food, clothing and car expenses

- 20% toward saving for major purposes

The balance of his salary and signing bonus and whatever else he earns goes to pay income taxes and to invest in long term income producing investments.

A substantial influence on his thinking besides his parents was the book *Rich Dad, Poor Dad* by Robert Kiyosaki. In his book, Kiyosaki teaches that earning a lot doesn't necessarily make you rich or that simply saving money doesn't make you financially free. "It's not how much money you make. It's how much money you keep," he writes. The rich not only save their money, but they put it to work by investing in long-term, income producing assets.

What are you going to do about what you just read in Step # 1? Write down how you could increase your income and/ or decrease your expenses so that you have a positive cash flow each month.

Step Two

AVOID ALL CONSUMER DEBT

Money is a great servant,
But a terrible master!

There is no such thing as good debt. Many people will argue this point and give examples where people have benefited from debt. While this may be the case in some instances, it is seldom a life of peace and tranquility to live with debt. People have won the lottery but that doesn't mean that you should adopt that as a FINANCIAL PHILOSOPHY.

The most common form of debt that people think is good debt is a mortgage on a house. While I agree that it may be a necessity if you want to own a home, I still believe that it should be paid down as fast as possible. Living without a mortgage is a wonderful experience. The best ways to accomplish this is to save up a good down payment, buy a modest house, incur a small mortgage and pay off the mortgage as soon as you can.

> ## IS MORTGAGE DEBT GOOD DEBT?
> ## ASK THE PEOPLE WHO LOST HOMES IN 2008-2010

Too often people buy the largest house that they can and plan to "grow" into it. When they get their next promotion or raise, then they will be all set. But what if that doesn't happen? You may end up losing that home and a whole lot more in the process. Losing a home is tough for most people to handle emotionally.

Secondly, student loans are touted as good debt. The idea is that it gives you an education that will allow you to earn more in the future. While this may be true about education, the idea of taking on student loans is not the best way to accomplish it. If you want an education then apply for scholarships, bursaries and grants from as many places as you can. These are easier to get than you may think. An innovative idea for a parent is to promise their child to match the scholarships, bursaries and grants up to a certain dollar amount. This really inspires a student to work hard at applying and obtaining them.

Another source of money for education is working during college years. It has been shown that students who work part time graduate better prepared for life than those who don't.

Why? A student who works must learn time management, money management and a greater level of personal responsibility than the student who doesn't have to work.

Thirdly, no form of consumer debt (such as credit cards, car loans or consumer loans) is ever a good idea. They all result from buying something that you couldn't afford to buy. These loans will end up incurring heavy interest charges. This means that you paid even more than you thought when you bought something using that debt. Debt consolidation loans are extremely dangerous. Most people who get them end up back in debt within one year.

A simple rule is that if you must borrow to buy something, then you cannot afford it right now. If you can't buy a car without borrowing, you should rethink it. Delay buying the car until you have saved enough to pay cash or buy a less expensive car until you have saved up the money for the car that you want. If you must charge a vacation or buy consumer products on a credit card and you don't have the savings to pay it off, then you can't afford them. Waiting until you can pay cash isn't popular but it is wise.

If you want to buy furniture or a car with zero percent interest or 90 days same as cash, don't fall for that trap. You will end up buying something that you can't afford. The reason the store offers "free" loans is that they know if you leave and think about it, you probably won't buy it. They want you to buy before you have a chance to think about it. You always end up paying more than you think that you are paying. Nobody in business gives you such a deal for "free".

REMEMBER, IF IT SOUNDS TOO GOOD TO BE TRUE, IT IS

The better the deal seems to you, the more you should take a second and third look at what is really going on. It is best to delay the purchase until you have talked to your financial advisor. That could save you a lot of money and a lot of headaches.

Once you have looked at the past and what your FINANCIAL PHILOSOPHY has been and where that has gotten you, you need to determine where you stand today. The key place to start is with your debts. List all your loans and the balance today. This doesn't have to be exact but as close as you can get. Use the list on the next page as an aid:

LIST OF LIABILITIES		
Order	Description	Amount
	VISA credit card	
	VISA credit card	
	MASTERCARD credit card	
	AMERICAN EXPRESS credit card	
	Other Credit Card	
	Store Credit Cards	
	Gas Credit Cards	
	Consumer loan - furniture	
	Consumer loan - electronics	
	Car loan # 1	
	Car loan # 2	
	Bill Consolidation Loan	
	Student Loans	
	Other loan	
	Other loan	
	Other loan	
	Other loan	
	TOTAL OF ALL CONSUMER DEBTS	
	1st Mortgage on home	
	2nd Mortgage on home	
	TOTAL OF ALL DEBTS	

For many people, this is an ugly surprise. The total debt that you owe may be much greater than you realized. Often the reason is that when you incur a loan, the lender will emphasize the low monthly payments rather than the total amount of the loan. You are probably not aware of the amount you owe.

How do you pay off your debts? It is simple:

> ## SPEND LESS THAN YOU EARN!

When you spend less than you earn, you have a surplus of cash every month. You can use the extra money to pay off your debts. Once you have paid off your old debts, you can use the extra money to save up to make major purchases that you need and save up for your retirement.

In the table above the left column is titled "ORDER". This is used to record the order in which you are going to pay off your debts.

Here are four ways that can help you pay off your consumer debts:

1. increase your income
2. decrease your expenses
3. both (1) and (2) above
4. sell assets that you own

The discussion of the first three techniques in the previous chapter is the same here. However, there is a fourth technique which is to "sell assets that you own". This simply means to make a list of all your assets and the value that you could get if you sold them. Once you have done this, look at the assets and determine if you really need them or not. Often people have assets such as boats and RV's which are not being used. Selling these has two benefits: it reduces maintenance and carrying costs such as insurance and registration plus it provides cash to pay down debt. Maybe there is some stock or a piece of real estate which you inherited that would be better sold and the proceeds used to pay down your debt. Remember that any money gained through the sale of assets is money that you don't have to earn to pay down your debts.

In addition to debt, look at the recurring costs that you have committed to paying each month such as gym membership and cell phone bills. While these are not liabilities, they are regular payments that you must make. In business, companies look at these long-term commitments like debts. Is there some way to reduce or eliminate these recurring debts?

Avoid All Consumer Debt

3 QUESTIONS THAT WILL TRANSFORM YOUR FINANCIAL LIFE

Let's look at 3 questions which may help you understand some of the current problems that you may be experiencing. If you look at some of the expenditures that you made in the last year or some of the debts that you incurred and ask yourself these questions, I think that you will see things differently.

Questions # 1 - What level of personal satisfaction did I receive from that expenditure?

- How do you feel about the purchase today?
- Weigh the cost with the level of satisfaction to see if it was worthwhile
- If you are making loan payments, how does that feel?
- Consider how long the "joy" lasted
- Examples: new car or expensive dinner at a restaurant

Questions # 2 - Was that purchase congruent with my stated values in life?

- Compare this purchase with your FINANCIAL PHILOSOPHY
- Did this purchase get you closer to your life goals?
- Did this purchase match your Life Plan?
- Did this give you more peace in your life?
- Example: buying a new sports car

Questions # 3 – Would I make this purchase if I was doing it today?

- Now you know the results

- Is there something of greater value that you would prefer?

- If you could, would you undo this purchase today?

- Example: can you return or sell the item and recover some of your money?

While I think that it is unhealthy to dwell on the mistakes of the past, I believe that it is extremely important to review your past to learn lessons that you can use in the future.

Why do you study history?

> **THE REASON THAT YOU STUDY HISTORY IS TO LEARN FROM THE MISTAKES (YOURS AND OTHERS) OF THE PAST AND MAKE BETTER DECISIONS TODAY.**

What do you learn from history?

> **MANY PEOPLE LEARN LITTLE FROM HISTORY, THEY MAKE THE SAME MISTAKES.**

- If you can look at your past and learn from your mistakes, then you will make better decisions today.

- If you can look at other people in history who have accomplished what you want to accomplish and learn from their example, then it will help you make better decisions today.

Although we are only talking about FINANCIAL FREEDOM in this book, this will apply to many areas of life.

EXAMPLE

John went to the car dealer just to look around with no intention of buying a new car but just to satisfy his curiosity. John saw an expensive sports car with a convertible roof. He fell in love with the sports car. Two hours later he left the dealership driving that beautiful new car. Was he happy? He was on cloud nine, he was in heaven, he was ecstatic. It was hard to describe how wonderful he felt driving that new car.

However, if you fast forward one year you see that John is not so happy with his purchase now. For starters, the monthly payment of $749.85 is hurting his cash flow. Next, John is very active outdoors kayaking, biking and golfing. His new sports car is not the best vehicle for carrying his kayak, bike or golf clubs not to mention his friends. He now must depend on other people to enjoy his outdoor sports. John and his wife have a six-month-old baby and a sports car is not the car for a family man. But John has another 4 years of loan payments. Yes, he could sell the car but that would mean taking a huge loss since cars lose a lot of their value in the first year.

Question # 1 Is John satisfied with his purchase?

Question # 2 Was the purchase congruent with John's values?

Question # 3 Would John make the purchase today?

Questions # 1 - What level of personal satisfaction did John receive from that expenditure?

> While John got a great deal of satisfaction from the "purchase" of the car and from driving it the first few months, this quickly diminished once he realized the limitations of the vehicle. The fact that he and his wife did not do this together was a major source of stress between them

Questions # 2 - Was the purchase congruent with John's stated values in life?

> The purchase of the car was not congruent with John's life values in several ways. The car did not carry his "toys". It did not carry his friends. It did not carry his family.

Questions # 3 – Would John make this purchase today?

> There is no way John would make this purchase if he had to make the decision today. While some decisions are easy to undo, this is one that will cost a lot of money to undo as well as cause friction between John and his wife.

THE TALE OF TWO HIGH SCHOOL CLASSMATES

It was the best of times,
It was the worst of times.

— Charles Dickens

Here are two stories about classmates in high school. These two boys learned from their parents and lived their lives based upon the values that their parents taught them. However, despite growing up in the same town at the same time, they have completely opposite results. See who you identify with and why.

JACK'S STORY

Jack grew up in a home with parents who lived a modest lifestyle. Jack's father worked hard at a blue-collar job. Jack's mother was a stay at home mom and looked after the kids, the house and the garden. The family did not incur any debt and only purchased what they could afford to buy with cash. That meant that they lived in a modest house and never moved, they owned a modest car which they kept for a long time and they wore modest clothes. They never went to Europe or Hawaii or any other exotic destination for vacations. They had a large vegetable garden so that they could enjoy fresh, nutritious produce and to reduce the cost of food.

Growing up in this family, it was only natural for Jack to learn and follow the family ways. Jack went to college and graduated with a degree in business and went into banking. Jack was a banker not only in his career but also in his personality. Jack said that he learned three valuable lessons from his parents which he used to guide his financial life:

- do not incur any debts

- save 10 % of everything that you earn

- be happy with what you have

Jack worked as a banker his whole career. He lived like his parents in that he owned a modest home, drove a used car, often took public transportation and incurred no debt except a mortgage on his home. He followed his father's advice and saved 10% of what he earned and invested it in mutual funds. He also took advantage of all tax advantaged saving programs.

What are the results of Jack adopting his parents' values? Jack lived a comfortable life and raised two fine sons. He retired at age 55 with a good pension from the bank and he had over $2,000,000 in mutual funds. Even though Jack retired at age 55, he still works part time at a job that he loves. He and his wife are free to travel all they want. They are enjoying a life full of FINANCIAL FREEDOM.

IAN'S STORY

Ian grew up in a much different home. His parents believed that they should live life to the fullest. They really wanted to impress their neighbors with what they possessed. His father was a car dealer so always drove a brand-new car. He owned a large home and the family moved several times when the family could "afford" to move to a better home. The family always went on expensive vacations and bought lots of new clothes and playthings.

Ian went off to college and graduated with a business degree. He looked around at the job prospects when he graduated and they were rather boring jobs working for other people. He wanted to be like his father and be his own boss. Therefore, he went on to law school and became a lawyer.

Ian and his family lived much like his parents did. They always drove a brand-new car, lived in the largest house that they could "afford" and spent lavishly. He lived his life by the rules which his father had taught him:

- debt is good because it can give you what you want NOW

- saving is a waste of time

- live life to the fullest now

What are the results of Ian's lifestyle? Today he continues to work even though he is past normal retirement age. He is ı debt not only with a mortgage on his house but consumer loans and credit card debt. He would like to retire but is unwilling to give up his lavish lifestyle to do it. Selling his large, expensive house and downsizing is not something that he is willing to do.

Although Ian made much more money in his working career than Jack did, he has a negative net worth and no chance of retiring under his present circumstances.

LIVING DEBT FREE IS TRUE FREEDOM

Do not a borrower be!

— Shakespeare

There are 3 basic types of debt that we will look at here:

1. consumer debt – credit cards, car loans, furniture loans, etc.
2. student loans
3. mortgage on your home

CONSUMER DEBT

Consumer debt is the worst kind of debt and should be avoided at all times. Consumer debt is based on things that were previously consumed (therefore the name consumer) or are in the process of being consumed rather quickly.

Incurring debt to buy clothes or furniture or vacations means that the second you buy the item, you have basically lost all the value of the item. You cannot sell them and get your money back. The interest rates typically are high on consumer debts because of the risk to the bank. Credit cards can have rates over 20% per year which means the amount will double in less than 5 years if not paid off. Credit card companies require a small minimum monthly payment which will keep you in debt because you will incur high interest costs.

Car loans are a little different. You own an asset that you could sell and pay down the loan. You probably couldn't pay off the loan because the car typically decreases in value faster than the loan balance decreases. Even zero percent interest loans are not a good deal because the dealer makes the interest in a higher price of the car up front. You should never have a car loan.

Car loans are one of the largest problems when it comes to consumer debt. Cars are depreciating assets so getting a loan on a car means that when the loan is paid off, there will be little value left in the car. There is one simple rule to follow when buying a car: always pay cash!

YOU SHOULD NEVER HAVE A CAR LOAN

What is the result of consumer debt? It is hard to feel free when the first portion of your paycheck must go to pay for past purchases. You are less free to spend your money the way that you wish today because you must keep paying for yesterday's purchases. This is doubly bad when yesterday's purchase was something like a boat or RV that looked good at the time but which is just sitting in your backyard wasting away. Instead of being an asset, the maintenance costs make it into a liability.

STUDENT LOANS

Many people refer to student loans as "good debt". This is because the loans allowed you to go to college and get an education which means that you can earn more today. This simply is not true.

You could go to college and not incur student loans and still have the same ability to earn more today. The advantage would be that you would not have to make student loan payments each month. If the value of the college education is something that you want, then it should be something that you are willing to find a way to pay for while you are going to college and not afterwards.

How can you go to college and not take on student loans?

- save before you go to college
- get parental help

- go to a junior college and then to an in-state school
- go to a local college and live at home
- get a job where your employer will pay for your education
- apply for scholarships (they are easier to get than most people think)
- apply for grants and bursaries
- apply to the college for financial aide
- get a job

Is getting a job such a terrible thing? Actually, it is a good thing. Studies have shown that students who work part time, develop better time and money management skills which are not only useful at college but in the work place also. Students with part time jobs average a grade level higher than their non-working peers because they are a little more serious about the money that is being spent on their education.

Students who don't work don't tend to study any harder or more than students who do work. They tend to play more and party more but generally these are not skills that are in much demand in the market place.

> ## YOU DON'T WANT TO START LIFE AFTER GRADUATION WITH STUDENT LOANS

MORTGAGE

Once you get to the point of having no debts you will know FINANCIAL FREEDOM. I have lived my life with no consumer debt but I had a mortgage on my home until I retired. I thought that I knew FINANCIAL FREEDOM because I didn't have any consumer debts. But, when I moved into my first mortgage free home, I couldn't believe it. For the past 10 years I have lived in a home with no mortgage and it is wonderful. Admittedly I live in a smaller home than I could if I wanted to take on a mortgage but now that I know how wonderful it is to be mortgage free, I would never want to buy a house where I would need to get a mortgage.

I understand that it is not easy to live completely debt free. But I recommend that you set that as a key goal in your financial plan. No one should ever have consumer debt of any kind. If you do currently I would recommend that you pay it off as soon as possible. I would also recommend that you set a definite plan to pay off your mortgage in a shorter time frame such as 5 or 10 years instead of 20 or 30 years.

While this point is not generally accepted as good practice, I would recommend it strongly. From an emotional point of view as well as a financial point of view, it is a worthwhile idea. People often argue that since mortgage interest is deductible on your tax return, it is good debt. However, the cost of the interest must be paid but only a fraction of that cost is returned on your tax return. It would be much better to not pay the interest and to lose the tax deduction.

I know the arguments for using financial leverage and I understand that they work great under certain circumstances. Financial leverage multiplies the returns on your investments. If they are positive, then you will get rich faster. However, if they are negative, then you will go broke a whole lot faster also. Financial leverage worked well for a lot of people before the 2008 crash of the real estate market.

Let's look at financial leverage and 3 stages of your financial life:

Stage # 1 - If you are young, then it may be an appropriate time to use financial leverage. In your 20's and 30's you can invest using financial leverage. If things don't work out, you have lots of time to recover.

Stage # 2 - If you are in your 40's and 50's, I would not recommend using financial leverage. You should be making good conservative investments for your retirement. This is the period when you should be paying down mortgages, increasing your savings and purchasing long-term income producing investments. During this period, your income is greater and your spending requirements are less.

Stage # 3 – In your 60's and up you should be living off the fruits of your investments. If you followed a good solid investment plan, you should have no debts including no mortgage and you should have a monthly investment income large enough to live on. You can retire from the job where you need to make a living. Now you can do volunteer work or work at a job that you want to work at even if the pay is not what you normally make.

I know a couple who started their financial plan when they were in their early 20's. He was a professional baseball player and she was an accountant. They struggled for a while when he was in the minor leagues and she was starting her career in accounting. But when he got his first big contract they sat down and developed a plan. A key idea was that the life of a professional athlete is not guaranteed to last a long time. He could play for 20 years or he could play a few years and either get injured or not be able to make the big money any more.

This couple decided to live on just 10% of his income and 50% of her income. The rest would be saved for their future. They lived quite well but not the glamorous life people envision a highly paid athlete could live. However, by the time they were in their mid 30's they were financially independent and could retire at any time. Their modest house was paid off, they had no debts of any kind and they had a significant investment portfolio. This was certainly not what most people in their situation would have done but it certainly worked well for them.

Once you get to the point that you are spending less than you earn and are debt free, then you can take that extra cash each month and invest in long term income producing assets.

CASH FLOW IS THE MOST IMPORTANT THING

SUCCESS STORY

A client of mine named George followed these first two strategies and is now a millionaire. During his working life, he never earned more than an average salary in his best year. However, it was what he did outside of work that made him his money.

When George started working he was a single man. He bought a house with four large bedrooms. He lived in the master suite and rented out the other three bedrooms. He charged himself rent for his bedroom also. In most cities and especially college towns there is always a demand for this type of accommodation. Every month he took all his rental income plus some additional money he could save and made the largest possible mortgage payment.

He also put the maximum amount that he could into tax deferred retirement plans.

He also incurred no consumer debt whatsoever. He drove an older car and kept it in good condition. He saved and paid cash for everything that he needed including major purchases.

After ten years he had his mortgage fully paid off. At this point he decided that he wanted to change his lifestyle so he sold his house which was not only mortgage free but also had appreciated in value over the ten years. He took the money and purchased a condo for cash and put the rest into mutual fund investments. Today, almost twenty years later, his stock market portfolio has a value of over $3,000,000.

George now lives a comfortable lifestyle in his mortgage free condo living with income from his pension, his tax deferred savings and his income producing asset of mutual fund investments. George still spends less than he earns but he is investing some of his money in building memories with his children and grand children. His latest adventure was to take them all on a vacation through Europe which I suspect they will remember for the rest of their lives.

What are you going to do about what you just read about in Step # 2?

Do you need a plan to pay off your current consumer debt?

Step Three

INVEST FOR
<u>YOUR</u> RETIREMENT

Most people do not prepare for retirement adequately. The result is that in the United States only 5% of retired people are financially independent and can truly enjoy their retirement. The other 95% must continue to work or live a very frugal life but not by choice.

> **MOST PEOPLE DO NOT PREPARE**
> **FOR RETIREMENT ADEQUATELY**

Most people do not save enough before retirement because they haven't mastered Step # 1 – Spend less than you earn every month. If you continually spend more than you earn every month, how can you save for retirement? During your working years, you must set aside a certain percentage of your income (10% or 20% or 50%) and invest this money in long term income producing assets than will pay you in retirement.

When would you prefer to make sacrifices in your life? You can make sacrifices before retirement by living a more modest lifestyle and saving money for retirement or you can make sacrifices during retirement by living a more modest lifestyle and saving money during retirement. The sacrifice before retirement is your choice but the sacrifice during retirement may not be your choice. Many people who spent freely during their working years life in poverty during their retirement years.

When you are in your 20's and 30's, it is extremely difficult for you to grasp the importance of saving for retirement. When you're in your 40's you start to wake up and realize that you should get started. When you reach your 50's and 60's you may realize that it is too late to save enough to retire. When you are in your 70's you may be working still hoping to retire some day. The main reason why people buy lottery tickets is so that they can overcome their bad decisions of the past.

There are very few companies today that give the old-style pension where you receive a certain amount every month. This is called a Defined Benefit Plan and is extremely costly for the employer.

Today, the most common type of pension plan is the Defined Contribution Plan. These pensions now are funded by you and/or by your employer. BUT you are responsible for SAVING your money and MANAGING your money. Since most people are not very good at these two skills, there is a growing problem that people will not realize until they retire. I believe that we are headed for major problems as more and more retired people find themselves worse off than when they were working.

How well you SAVE and MANAGE your money will determine how much you enjoy or don't enjoy your retirement years. Since most people don't understand financial planning enough, this makes Defined Contribution Pensions very risky in the long term. If you mismanage your retirement funds, you may end up going back to work or end up broke.

"I can always live of my Social Security benefits, right?" Absolutely not! Social Security is a supplement that is meant to assist you so that you don't starve in your senior years. It was never meant to be a pension plan and you would not want to live on the money that you receive from Social Security.

SOCIAL SECURITY IS NOT A PENSION

Retirement was originally meant to be very short, just a few years. The retirement age of 65 was picked when the average life expectancy was 55 years. That meant that very few people reached retirement age and received pension benefits. Of those who made it, they died very shortly after their 65th birthday so didn't collect the pension for very long. However, today average life expectancy has increased from 55 to 77 for men. However, if you are 60 years old and still in good health, the odds of you living to be 100 years old are very good. That means that almost everyone gets a pension for a long time. The pension systems and especially the Social Security system were not designed for this change. Many pension plans are facing a shortage of funds to pay out pensions for such a long period of time.

YOU ARE RESPONSIBLE FOR YOUR RETIREMENT

After you have paid off all your consumer debt, you can start saving for retirement. You need to invest in income producing assets. It doesn't matter what they are so long as they meet your criteria. What are your criteria? Here are a few suggestions:

- the money should have minimal risk
- the funds should earn a return higher than the rate of inflation
- there should be some flexibility on transfers

Here are some ways to get started:

1. purchase a home that pays you income each month. This could be one where you rent rooms or a home with a separate unit that you can rent. Obviously, there is an

element of work managing the property and a certain amount of loss to your personal privacy but from a financial point of view this yields amazing results.

2. invest in employer sponsored tax-advantaged retirement programs like 401(k) or 403 (b). If there is dollar for dollar matching by the employer, you should always invest up to the matching limit at least. A dollar for dollar matching gives you more than 100% return in the first year. But you should always maximize your contributions annually.

3. invest in tax-advantaged retirement programs like an IRA. There are various programs such as Traditional IRA, SEP IRA and SIMPLE IRA. Each one has its own rules and restrictions. See which one is best for you and invest the maximum every year.

4. invest in a ROTH IRA. I separated this from the tax deferred programs because this is a much different type of program. Unlike the other IRA programs, this one uses after tax dollars and TAX-FREE income in retirement. With the prospect of higher tax rates in the future, you should give this thoughtful consideration.

5. purchase a life insurance policy such as an Indexed Universal Life policy. You can use such a policy to hold cash for later in life and you can get the benefits before you die. This will give you insurance protection and best of all TAX-FREE income during your retirement

years. With the prospect of higher tax rates in the future, you should give this earnest consideration.

6. invest in rental real estate. Rental property can provide a stable source of income that will adjust with inflation. Investment property is a business so there will be management and maintenance requirements. If you're not sure where to start, consider reading books on real estate investing but don't go out and start investing in real estate without doing your homework. Sometimes people jump on the real estate bandwagon simply because they knew a friend or neighbor who did very well with real estate. Real estate is not very liquid so that is a key factor to consider when investing.

7. invest in mutual funds. I strongly recommend that you DON'T invest in the stock market yourself. You would be a very small fish in a very big ocean and you would probably get eaten up over time. Investing in mutual funds is much less risky because you have a team of trained professionals managing the funds. Also, the mutual funds are large enough to make major purchases in which you would not be able to get involved.

8. start a part time business that you enjoy and that you can operate during retirement. For example, a pet sitting business, travel agent, driving a taxi, catering, tourist guide, etc. Pick something that you enjoy doing.

Invest In Income Producing Assets

The ideal situation is that you start to invest in income producing assets early in life. Every year you work for your salary and you receive income from your income producing assets. You save and invest part of your salary and you reinvest 100% of your income from your income producing assets. This provides a snowball effect and your savings will grow dramatically.

Here is something that people don't realize is possible. The retirement age was a completely random number when it was originally picked. No one has really challenged the idea since. If you save enough and make wise investments, you don't have to retire at 65 but maybe at 55 or 45. Many people in Silicon Valley are able to retire in their 30's. It is wonderful to be able to retire early. Everyone I know who retired early is glad that they did. Many of them still work but at a job that they enjoy rather than one that makes them the most money. It really does not take a lot to get to that point where you can retire. But you must live within your means and SAVE first and that is the basic problem in the United States today. People do not save. The current savings rate is under 4% in the United States. This means that for all the money that a person earns, they save less than 4% of that income. To save a significant amount for retirement takes a much larger savings rate.

To put that into perspective, with a 4% saving rate it would take you 25 years to save up one year's salary. After 50 years of work you would only have saved two year's salary. That means that you could retire for about two years. It certainly wouldn't fund a long retirement. Today, individuals who reach age 60 without any major illness, have a high probability of living until they are 100 years old. That means that you need enough income in retirement to last 35 years.

> ## SAVING IS THE CORNERSTONE
> ## OF YOUR RETIREMENT PLAN

Here is another problem when you are retired. You must pay taxes! You will probably have to pay taxes on your Social Security. You will have to pay taxes on any salary that you earn during retirement years. You will have to pay taxes on any money that you receive from a pension plan. You will have to pay taxes on any money that you take out of a 401(k), 403(b) or IRA account (except for a ROTH IRA). These accounts are not TAX FREE as some people believe but instead are TAX-DEFERRED. This means that you don't pay taxes when the money is going into the accounts but when the money comes out of the accounts in retirement. This means if you want to receive $50,000 to live on, you will have to take from your IRA approximately $72,000 assuming a 30% tax rate.

What do you think tax rates will be when you retire? For the past 30 years tax rates have been low compared to historical rates. The highest tax rate today is under 40%. In the 1950's and 1960's the top tax rates were over 90%. What do you think the tax rates will be when you retire? There is a compelling argument that tax rates will go up in the future and if history is any indicator, they could possibly double.

The number one problem that we face in the United States is the National Debt which currently stands around $20 Trillion. That is an inconceivable amount and doesn't count all the government's hidden obligations in the form of guaranteed payments which add an additional $60 Trillion. How can the United States pay back such a considerable sum of money? The government seems incapable of balancing a budget (equivalent to Step # 1) never mind having a surplus to pay back the loan.

TAX RATES MAY BE HIGHER IN THE FUTURE

At some point in the future this will become a crisis because the government will be unable to pay its debts. The government at that point will have only two choices. The government could print more money and pay the debts but this would cause high inflation rates. Or the government could raise income tax rates and use the extra money to pay down the National Debt. Based upon history, tax rates have risen after a war caused the National Debt to rise and then were lowered after the National Debt was paid down to a reasonable level. Therefore, I believe that we can expect higher tax rates in the future.

Many people continue to work in their retirement years for many reasons including:

- provides income

- provides health benefits

- provides structure to their lives

- gives them a sense of accomplishment

- gives them a sense of satisfaction

- provides social interaction

- allows them to do something that they couldn't do when they were younger

If you live on your regular income and save most of your extra income, it will greatly shorten the period before you are able to retire. Remember that as soon as your investments are providing enough income for you to live on, you can retire from your regular job. You don't have to retire of course but you are free to retire if you want. The longer you continue to work and have extra income, the more that you will save and the better your future standard of living.

It is best if you set a goal of retiring at a certain age and then make a financial plan to be financially independent at that age. I set the age of 55 to retire as my goal very early in life. I worked towards that goal and did retire at 55 and was able to live on my pension and investments. In retirement, I am not content sitting around doing nothing. I like golf, riding my bike and hiking but not every day. Since I retired I have continued to do consulting work on a part-time basis. This way I can enjoy playing and I can be stimulated by my work. More recently, I opened an income tax business and I enjoy the work and the people I interact with in my business.

This is not meant to be a detailed plan of how to invest for retirement but just a word of encouragement to get you started. I would recommend that you use a trusted financial advisor to guide you with your investments. No one is smart enough to know everything about investing. If you are your own financial advisor, you are not objective and may make bad decisions. Financial decisions should be made from a logical, rational basis. Too often people who are their own financial advisor make emotional decisions that end up hurting them. If you need a recommendation for a financial advisor, contact me and I will help you out. I know several trustworthy investment advisors that I could recommend to you.

FINANCIAL PLANNER

Should you use a financial planner? That is a question that many people ask. The answer is "YES" that you should use a TRUSTWORTHY financial planner. The trick is not to find a financial planner but to find one who will work in your best interests.

Too many who put themselves out as financial planners are not trained to give you good financial advice on your overall financial situation.

- Often, they are trained to sell a financial product and they can't advise you beyond that one area of investing.

- Many are paid commissions on what you do with your money. This leads them to direct you into investments that are best for them

- Some make commissions on every trade that is made with your money. This leads to a lot of activity in your account but not much benefit to you.

- Some don't know about strategies that will reduce your tax position now or in the future.

I am not against financial planners at all. I believe that you should have a team of financial advisers. The financial planner is like the quarterback of that team who plans for your future and coordinates the efforts of the other players — accountant, tax preparer, banker, mortgage broker, insurance agent, trust lawyer – to give you the best possible outcome. You could do this yourself but you probably don't know enough about finances. Accountants and tax preparers are often asked for financial advice but they tend to focus more on your past than your future. Besides, their advice will probably be limited to income tax strategies and not really investment strategies.

I strongly recommend that you find a good financial planner. The reasons why I say this include:

- a planner is trained in finances

- a planner knows the best ways to prepare for retirement

- a planner is objective and is not making emotional decisions

- a planner can determine what is best for you by seeing all parts of your finances

- a planner will be available long term to manage your money in the growth phase and the retirement phase

- a planner is critical at the time of divorce and the separation of assets

- a planner will think of the things that you don't want to think about like illness, injury, long term care and death

- a planner should be the first person you call if you receive a large amount of money for any reason – inheritance, lottery winning, bonus, etc.

- a planner should be consulted before any large financial transactions like purchasing a home, buying a car, withdrawing money from investments, etc.

- a planner will help plan your estate and how it will affect you, your children and your grandchildren

- a planner will coordinate your financial team

How do you pick a good financial planner? Ask your current financial professionals for recommendations. Ask your friends who are financially successful for a referral. Interview several financial planners to determine if their values are a match to yours.

Typically, financial planners charge a percentage of your portfolio as a management fee. This should be all they get to keep them objective. If they are getting commissions or referral fees or "kickbacks" then they are not the one for you.

SUCCESS STORY

A client named Brad used this three-step approach to FINANCIAL FREEDOM to be able to retire at age 42. Brad's story starts at age 25 when he graduated from college. He had spent three years in the Marines before going to college.

At age 25, Brad decided that he wanted to retire at age 55 with enough money to experience FINANCIAL

FREEDOM. When he started work he started using this three-step approach. First, he spent less than he earned each month. He avoided all consumer debt and he invested in long term income producing assets. He saved up for all major purchases so that he paid cash for everything including his car. He follows my recommendation of not paying more than $5,000 for an automobile and has been very successful with it.

For his investment strategy, he used two different investments. First, he invested the maximum amounts into income tax deferred programs. He put them into mutual funds but where he had flexibility to move money around as he saw fit.

The second investment was in rental real estate. He purchased a condo, then a single-family home, then another condo and then two fixer upper homes. This happened over the period of about ten years and took time to research, find the properties, find the financing, get the properties ready to rent and then manage the renters. This was all done in addition to his regular job. This was a sacrifice of time and effort but the long-term results were wonderful.

At age 42 Brad was in a position where his cash flow from the real estate gave him enough that he no longer needed to work. He quit his high stress job in San Jose, California and moved to a mountain town in Utah where he could ski and mountain bike, his two favorite hobbies. He still works part time but at a job that he enjoys. His commute is five minutes instead of an hour as it was in San Jose. He can easily manage his rental properties from where he lives.

If you asked Brad if it was a huge sacrifice, he would say no. Yes, there were sacrifices but nothing compared to the pleasure of retiring at age 42 after just seventeen years of work. Many people spend 30 or 40 years of work and retire with a meager pension. He retired after 17 years with enough investment income to live in FINANCIAL FREEDOM.

What are you going to do about what you just read in Step # 3?

What is your first investment for retirement going to be?

Section Three:

ADDITIONAL FINANCIAL IDEAS

If you manage
Your money,
You will always
Have enough!

Idea One

SAVE FOR AN EMERGENCY FUND

What would you do if you had to pay $5,000 for car repairs tomorrow?

What would you do if you had to pay $10,000 in advance for emergency medical services tomorrow?

What would you do if you couldn't work for a month or two?

For most people, this would mean going into debt. For some it could mean going into bankruptcy. In general, people are not prepared for emergencies and there is one thing that we can be assured of in life: EMERGENCIES HAPPEN.

Here are a few advantages of using an Emergency Fund:

- it gives you a sense of security
- you are prepared for an emergency so you avoid some of the stress that might go along with it

- you will not make poor decisions when you must raise money quickly. Whenever you are forced to borrow or to sell assets during a time of an emergency, you will not get the best result.

One of the most amazing parts of FINANCIAL FREEDOM is feeling free. This gives you PEACE which is truly priceless. If an emergency arises, people who are financially free have the resources to pay for these events. One way to do this is through saving with the use of an Emergency Fund.

How do you hold the money in an Emergency Fund? A simple approach is to set aside in a Certificate of Deposit (CD) an amount and don't cash it in except for an emergency. A CD is easy to cash when needed but is separate from all other money so not easy to dip into for the wrong reasons.

How do you determine what amount should be in your Emergency Fund? You can use an arbitrary amount of $10,000. Many people use a guideline of three, six or twelve months of expenses to save in their emergency fund. Knowing there is money sitting there for emergencies is a great comfort.

If you do not have an Emergency Fund, how are you going to pay for an emergency when it arises? Here are a few ways NOT to pay for emergencies:

- take a cash advance on your credit card. This usually involves a fee of about 3% plus interest of over 20%.

- withdraw money from your tax deferred retirement account. This involves a 10% penalty if you are under 59½ years old. In addition, you must pay tax at your marginal tax rate.

- borrow from family and friends. When you borrow from family and friends, you are changing the nature of the relationship to lender and borrower. Usually that is not conducive to good long-term relationships.

- sell assets under duress. If you have an asset that is not readily liquid and you must sell it in a hurry, you usually don't get what it is worth.

Brian Tracy, the great motivational speaker and author, tells the story of one time in his career when he set aside $10,000 and it changed the way he thought about money. He had lost his business and he had to sell everything that he owned including his home. After selling everything and paying off all his creditors, there was $10,000 left over. He wanted to use this to start a new business. However, his wife felt that they should set it aside in an Emergency Fund. He put the $10,000 into a CD. He states that knowing that that money was there if an emergency arose gave him a profound sense of security and peace. He has never touched that money to this day.

I recommend that you make having an Emergency Fund a part of your FINANCIAL PHILOSOPHY.

Idea Two

GIVE 10% TO CHARITY

What you sow, you shall reap

Giving to a charity or church means that you are helping people who are worse off than you are. Despite how bad you may feel or what troubles you may be going through, there are many people who are much worse off than you.

**BEING POOR IN THE UNITED STATES
MAKES YOU BETTER OFF THAN MOST PEOPLE
IN THE ENTIRE WORLD**

You benefit in many ways when you give. Here is a list of benefits that come from giving:

- the gift benefits the recipient
- the gift has a ripple effect and affects even more people down the line

- giving is good for your health

- giving usually results in receiving but not from the person to whom you gave

- giving makes you feel happier

- giving promotes cooperation and social connection

- giving evokes the feeling of gratitude in both the giver and receiver

- giving also helps you keep money in its proper perspective

- giving influences other people to give

- giving may be directly related to your income. The more you give, the more you will receive

- giving unleashes power in your life

Here are a few people who were big givers:

- Andrew Carnegie was the second richest man in the world when he retired in 1870. He felt that it was his duty to give his money away so in the next ten years he gave away ninety percent of his fortune. He is mostly remembered for building over three thousand libraries at a time when books were not readily available to the average person.

- Robert Morris lived at the time of the Revolutionary War. He was an extremely rich man. He donated money to finance a large part of the expenses of the Continental Army. It is said that without his help, the American Colonies would have lost the war effort and not obtained their independence from Britain. It is hard to estimate the amount that he paid but it affected his financial situation considerably. Just think where the United States would be today if the Continental Army had lost to England.

- Warren Buffet has pledged to give away 99% of his wealth to charity. He is the richest man in the world so consider the impact that he will have.

- Bill Gates and his wife Melinda Gates have set up a charitable foundation and are donating most of their fortune to the foundation.

- In addition to donating his own fortune, Bill Gates has joined with 14 other billionaires who are giving at least 50% of their fortunes to the Bill & Melinda Gates Foundation.

I recommend that you make giving a significant amount every year a part of your FINANCIAL PHILOSOPHY.

Idea Three

PAY CASH FOR ALL PURCHASES

This may be the most unpopular idea expressed in this book. To pay cash for all major purchases you must save the cash before you purchase. That means delaying the purchase. This goes against our society's thinking about major purchases. Today credit cards or some form of consumer debt can be used to purchase anything you want right now!

It is not uncommon to hear about someone who went out with no intention of buying anything and then returning with a new car or television or some large purchase. Buying on credit is so easy that almost anyone can do it. Car dealers regularly advertise no money down to buy or lease a car. Sellers usually emphasize the "small monthly payment" over the actual full cost or loan balance.

Once you are debt free, you can use your monthly savings for retirement but you can also use some of that money for major purchases. Start a savings account which you use to save for major purchases. Don't be watching the fund but just put the money aside. When you need something like a new car or new appliance, then you have money set aside to make the purchase with cash. If you want to buy a new car or appliance, these do not constitute an emergency so you don't get to access your Emergency Fund.

The advantages of using cash to make all major purchases:

- you will get a better price

- you will have a better negotiating position

- there will be no monthly loan payments for the next few years

- you delay long enough to realize that you don't really want this item

- you are likely to find a way to save cash such as buying a used item instead of a new one

- once you have purchased the item with cash, you will be free to just enjoy the item with no loan to deal with

- there is a strange sense of pride when you make a purchase for cash

It is a very old fashion way of doing things but one that is extremely valuable. Before easy credit started about seventy years ago, this is how all major purchases were made.

Paying cash for purchases will have many benefits but there are two that I would like to emphasize here:

1. The emotional benefit of a good financial decision is often overlooked but is extremely important. When you buy on credit it can lead to a lot of stress from having to make monthly payments to facing bankruptcy. This stress can affect an individual but really affects a couple. If you are having troubles with your finances, it is probable that you are having trouble with your relationship also.

2. There will be tremendous savings from paying cash for everything. When you save up and pay cash, it slows down the whole purchasing cycle. This leads to more time to think about the decision and research alternatives. The result is often a better decision such as "this is not a good idea" to "let's buy a used item and save". It is not an accident that when you use a credit card you spend more because there is a disconnect between the card and cash. But when you spend your own cash that you took time to save up, you have a better feel for the cost of the purchase and therefore you are going to be much more diligent with your money.

I recommend that you make paying cash for all purchases a part of your FINANCIAL PHILOSOPHY.

Idea Four

PAY CASH WHEN YOU BUY A CAR

How do you save money on a vehicle?

- buy a new car and keep it for a long time
- buy a good used car and maintain it. For many people, purchasing a good used car is better than buying a new car.

I believe that buying new cars is one of the greatest financial problems in our country. For the past sixty years, the car manufacturers have spent billions of dollars on advertising to convince you that you need to buy a new car. They want you to believe that it is okay to buy a new car and that you deserve it. If you watch sports on television, there is a significant percentage of the advertisements that are about buying a new car or pickup truck.

The commercials always show the fun or the prestige of owning a new vehicle. But they never show the cost. There will be years of paying car payments which go on long after the thrill of the new vehicle has gone. There are higher insurance payments and registrations fees for new vehicles than for older ones. New vehicles are not without their problems. It can be just as expensive to maintain a new vehicle as a used vehicle.

I also recommend that you buy a car from a private seller instead of a dealer. The owner selling the car knows the car best. If you talk to the seller and get a feel for his level of integrity, you can feel good about buying the vehicle. Private individuals are selling their old car because it doesn't meet their needs anymore. Dealers are selling to make a profit. A dealer may tell you that you are buying a great used car and that they fixed it up. But are they going to back it up with any meaningful guarantee or warranty on the vehicle?

I have had a personal philosophy of not spending more than $5,000 on a vehicle. I am not suggesting that you adopt my philosophy. But think about and set up a philosophy that works for you. Women tend to prefer to buy newer cars than older because they don't want to get stranded or deal with repairs. I can see their point but there is a cost for that method.

Buying a good used car for under $5,000 is kind of a game for me. I have only once paid more than $5,000 for a car or truck. I have usually driven Toyota 4Runners or Lexus vehicles because they are well built and require very little maintenance. Today, I drive a nice Ford F-150 that I purchased for $4,000. One of the big advantages of buying cars like this is that they depreciate very little. I can buy a Toyota 4Runner for $3,500 and drive it for two years and then sell it again for about what I paid for it. I budget $1,000 for preventative maintenance and routine upkeep each year because I want to keep my vehicle in top shape. This may sound high to you but it is a lot less than the payments that someone makes on a new car.

Cars today are built to last a lot longer than they used to be. If you have a good car, keep it longer. Budget an amount to spend each year keeping it in top running condition. If you must spend more than you are comfortable with, it may be time to get rid of the car.

In case you are wondering, I am NOT a mechanic. In fact, I have NO mechanical skills. I do nothing to the cars myself including I don't even wash them myself. I will tell you the trick of buying a good used car:

DON'T BUY THE CAR, BUY THE SELLER

Here is how I usually buy a car. I decide what I want and I go on Craigslist and find the car. I recommend a large population center like San Francisco Bay area because there are lots of vehicles to choose from. I also recommend areas where cars have not been exposed to severe weather conditions. I always buy from a private party and not from anyone who is in the business of selling cars. I "interview" the seller/owner of the car to find out what he is like, what the history of the vehicle is and the reason for selling it. If he seems like a good honest person and he has owned the car for a long time and kept it well maintained and his reason for selling sounds reasonable, I will buy the car. I am not looking for the lowest price but the best vehicle at a reasonable price. I only purchased one bad car in my life and that was when I was 16 years old and relied upon my father's advice.

Here is a general rule for buying cars:

> ### *ALWAYS PAY CASH FOR YOUR CAR!*

A client asked my advice on what type of car she should buy. I asked her,

"How much money do you have saved for a car?"

She answered, "$5,000."

I told her that she should buy a $5,000 car. You can only afford the car that you can buy with the cash you have.

If you have $15,000 or $50,000 saved to spend on a car, then go ahead and buy a car for cash. But don't borrow to buy a car. That means that you are buying a car that you can't afford.

NEVER BORROW TO BUY A CAR

Some people will argue that buying used cars is risky and I agree that it can be. They argue that it is best to buy a new car and keep it for a long time. That is a valid argument if you pay cash for that new car. A 0% loan is not the same as cash! Don't fall into that trap.

Here is a word of warning about buying a new car using a car loan. Let's say that you have your heart set on a brand new $50,000 car. If you finance it, all you see is the monthly payment of $999. You think that you can afford that not realizing that it is going to be for the next 5 to 7 years and long after the newness of the car has worn off.

But if you take your $50,000 in cash that you saved down to buy the car, there is a good chance that you will change your mind and not buy that car. Why? Because you will feel the pain of spending so much hard-earned money on a car and you will likely make a better decision and buy a cheaper car. While the loan payment of $999 sounds much better than spending $50,000 in cash, it camouflages the true cost of the vehicle.

Here is a key point about cars. They will depreciate over time. They will decrease in value over time. Therefore, you need to be aware that most of what you spend on a car will be lost. If you buy a $50,000 car, some day it will be worth $5,000. If you buy a $5,000 car, how much do you have to lose?

There is one last point to remember about your car and your house. Your self worth is not in any way determined by your car or house. Too many people drive cars to impress others, usually people who they don't even know. Many people have houses that are too big and expensive, so that when they host Christmas dinner, everyone in the family will be impressed. If you do either of these, you are paying a high price for nothing. It would be better to buy a smaller and cheaper house or car.

Many people who are rich still drive older cars. For example, Sam Walton was worth billions but still drove his old pickup truck that he had owned for years. Warren Buffet is also worth billions but still drives an old Cadillac that he has owned for years. Being a wise steward of your money will lead you to a richer life in many ways.

While I talk about paying under $5,000 for a car, many people find this idea rather extreme and I fully understand. I suggest that you pick a number that you are comfortable with and use that as your limit. Some people use $10,000 or $15,000 as the limit. It doesn't matter so much what your limit is but the fact that you start with a limit. Make it a game and see what you can purchase under your limit. You will be pleasantly surprised.

I recommend that you make paying cash when you buy a car a part of your FINANCIAL PHILOSOPHY.

Idea Five

GET AN ADVISOR FOR MAJOR PURCHASES

Making larger purchases is a problem for many people. Any purchase that you make which is not a part of your routine spending needs to be handled differently. When you shop for groceries, clothes, gas, etc., you know what you are doing. But when you shop for other items (like computers, TV's, cars, furniture, vacations, etc.) you may get into trouble. You may make your decision to purchase based too much upon emotion and too little upon rational thinking.

I recommend that before you make any purchase over $1,000, that you stop and think about it first and wait one or two days. I am not saying don't do it or that you must ask for permission. I am just saying stop and treat it as something special and give it some thought and some time. This simple act will save you lots of money over time. I strongly recommend that you find someone to act as your advisor in these situations. Asking them will get an objective opinion and delay the purchase for a day or two. This delay might just make you realize that you don't really want that thing after all.

Every decision you make in life has two components: emotional and rational thinking. A good decision will have some of both. For example, when you buy a car, you don't want it to be a 100% rational decision because you won't like the car when you must drive it every day. On the other hand, you don't want it to be a 100% emotional decision because you may not have a car that is very practical or you might have a large loan payment that you don't like. A wise decision will be a blend of emotional and rational thinking.

BALANCE EMOTIONAL AND RATIONAL THINKING

Here are a few guidelines for making larger purchases:

- take your time to make the decision (think it over for a few days)

- do research to ensure that you buy the right product for your needs

- ask advice from a trusted friend or financial advisor

- balance what you want with what is best in the circumstances

- always pay cash for any large purchase

- talk it over with two or three people and then consider their input

- don't decide today but wait a few days

- don't decide today but wait until your emotional excitement dies down

- don't get pressured into buying because the "sale" is going to expire

I personally have a policy that if I am thinking of spending over $1,000 I will talk it over first with two of my good friends. They have saved me a lot of money over the years. Before I adopted this policy, I made my buying decisions too often using emotional and not rational thinking. When I have an idea, I phone them and talk it over with them. First, it delays deciding which eliminates impulsive buying. Secondly, if it makes sense to them I feel better about the decision. But if it doesn't make sense to them, then I will postpone the decision and think it over considering their input. Remember you are not asking for their permission but just seeking their opinion and wisdom in the situation. Many times, I have found that I ended up not spending the money.

Many people hate to ask for advice and want to be able to make their own decisions. But I would strongly recommend that you find one or two people who will guide you through these situations. Be sure to ask people who are DOING

WELL FINANCIALLY and obviously make good financial decisions. I recommend friends or financial advisors over relatives because they can be more objective and there is less chance for other emotional issues to interfere with the advice. That is not to say that your relatives should not be asked but I would just exercise some caution in deciding who you choose.

Using financial advisors has another benefit. When you are negotiating, you can honestly say that you are not able to make the decision right now. This eliminates impulse buying and being pressured into a bad purchase.

I recommend that you make getting an advisor for major purchases a part of your FINANCIAL PHILOSOPHY.

Idea Six

PURCHASE A MODEST HOME

The typical American way of buying a house is to purchase the biggest house that you can afford now or maybe not afford now but in the near future. Many people will assume that they will get raises in the future and so will be able to afford this house. They also assume that nothing will go wrong with this house or their finances.

Buying like this is living on the edge financially speaking. What could go wrong?

- you could lose your job after buying a house
- you could get pregnant and the second paycheck goes away
- you could get sick or injured and be unable to work for some period
- the economy could go into a slowdown
- the house could require some major repairs

It is often assumed that house prices will always increase so it is wise to buy the biggest house possible since it will appreciate the most. As we saw last decade, housing prices can drop and when they do, it is hard to get out without losing money.

If you purchase a modest home, the cost of maintaining it will be less. The risk of losing it will be less. People won't want to rob you as much as the nicer house that is down the street.

Did you read the book titled *Millionaire Next Door*? You might remember that many wealthy people bought a modest home in a nice neighborhood and stayed there for a very long time. They lived there long after they could afford a more expensive home. This is one of the ways that they got rich. Staying in the same house for a long time minimizes the cost of housing. It also leads to a more peaceful life.

Who did this? Warren Buffet lives in a modest house and only owns one house. He purchased his house in 1958 and still lives in the same house. When asked why he doesn't have homes around the world he said,

"In some cases, I feel the possessions possess their owner, rather than the other way around."

When asked why he hadn't upgraded to a more expensive home, he answered,

"I'm happy here. I'd move if I thought I'd be happier someplace else".

For most people, buying a home is the single most important financial decision that you will ever make. If you think in terms of investing in a home instead of buying a home, I believe that you will do much better financially. In most areas of the United States I believe that it is best to own your own home. However, in certain high cost areas this may not prove to be true. But usually the cost of owning is about the same as renting but with additional advantages.

A client of mine who is retired has not paid for housing in his whole life. Instead he put all the money he saved into buying a house and paying it off. Today he lives in a million-dollar home which is mortgage free and it provides part of his retirement income. I will use his philosophy as a model for this chapter.

How did he do it? My client started out when he was in his 20's. He purchased a house that had several big bedrooms. He rented out the bedrooms that he did not need. He could collect enough money to pay his mortgage, taxes, insurance and utilities. He could live for free in this house. But he also paid himself rent for his bedroom and put that as extra mortgage payments. It did not take him long to pay down his mortgage significantly.

Next, he bought a house that had several bedrooms and a basement apartment. Now he could rent out the apartment and the extra bedrooms and make even more income. He still paid himself rent which he put towards the mortgage.

Today, he lives in a beautiful home in an exclusive area. Although it is a million-dollar home, he has no mortgage on it. Plus, he has two rental apartments in the house. He lives in this beautiful home and has two rents coming in every month which is part of his retirement income.

In most of the United States, this is not hard to do but you must be willing to make certain sacrifices. I bought a small home a few years ago for cash. I then divided it in two and rented out one half. I, lived in the other half for free. Later I decided to rent out both halves of the house. It doesn't take too much imagination to generate some income from real estate.

Housing is the biggest expense for most people. If you are willing to share a house in some way, you will be better off financially. It doesn't have to be forever. In many areas, there are duplexes (or triplexes or fourplexes) available where you can live in one part and rent out the other. There may also be some large houses that you could buy and rent out the bedrooms that you are not using.

If you want to live in your own home, then don't buy the biggest house that you can afford or that you can get into today. I believe that you will be much happier with a smaller house that has a smaller mortgage (or no mortgage) and smaller operating costs. Many people who have large houses use over half the house for storage of their "stuff" that they never use. When I ask people why they own such large homes, they often say that it is because they like to have parties. If that is true, how much is it costing to have parties? They could easily rent a facility and host the party there. The advantage of renting is that they could have parties in various locations which would be more interesting.

Where I live the average house costs over $1,000,000. It seems crazy to me to have that much sitting in a house. That much money could buy rental properties that will generate cash flow instead of your home which usually decreases cash flow.

It doesn't make sense to buy a house and pay enormous amounts to live each month when buying a more modest house and getting some rental income would give you the ability to pay off the mortgage sooner. While it may seem like a hardship to be living in a modest or shared house, you will find it wonderful when you can retire at a younger age or do more in retirement because you are financially free.

Be careful of buying a house because you feel that it will appreciate. While this is a good thing, you must sell the house to get that appreciation. Buy the house that you like to live in and if you stay a long time, it doesn't matter if it appreciates because it is your home.

I strongly recommend that you look at "investing" in a home that you can live in today but will lead you to a much better life down the road.

I recommend that you make purchasing a modest home a part of your FINANCIAL PHILOSOPHY.

Idea Seven

PAY OFF YOUR MORTGAGE EARLY

When discussing personal finances there are two critical aspects but one is usually overlooked. First there is the financial piece and secondly there is the emotional piece. Most people overlook the emotional piece thinking that it is unimportant. But, the emotional piece determines how happy you are, how well you get along with people and how well you sleep, very important parts of life. If you feel financial stress, it doesn't matter how good a deal it is, it is stressful and often not worth the stress.

Paying off your mortgage is more of an emotional decision that a financial decision. While it is a good financial decision, it will be the emotional benefits that you will appreciate the most. If you live in a mortgage free house, you view life a whole lot differently. Most people in California spend between 25% and 50% of their monthly income on their mortgage or rent payment. Just think that if they lived in a mortgage free house, they would have more money available for other things. Or, to look at it another way, if you don't have to make a mortgage or rent payment when you retire, you don't need as much monthly income. That means that you could retire sooner because you don't have to save as much for retirement.

Many advisors would disagree with paying off your mortgage before you save for retirement. I believe paying off your mortgage and owning a house that is mortgage free is one of the most financially freeing things that you can do. Even if you don't have a good pension, if you have a debt free house you won't need as much income to live comfortably.

Another argument for not paying off your mortgage is that the interest is tax deductible. I have known people who were advised to buy a big, expensive home so that they would get the mortgage interest deduction. For every dollar you spend in interest, you get less than forty cents back (depending on your marginal tax rate). I just don't know how spending a dollar to get forty cents is ever going to make you financially free.

When you buy a house always plan to pay it off in 10 or 15 years. No matter what type of mortgage you get, be sure that you can make additional principal payments whenever you like. That way you will save a little extra every month and save a lot of money over the life of the house. Usually the mortgage interest will be more than the cost of the house by the time it is paid off. You can save and prepare for retirement a lot better if you pay off your mortgage in the shortest time possible.

If you are interested in paying off your mortgage, there are many ways of doing it. Don't pay someone to do it for you! Do a little research and then figure which method works best for you and then follow it. It is easy to take your 30-year mortgage and calculate how much additional payment it would take each month to pay it off sooner.

If you got a second job or did something on the side to earn extra income and you put all the income towards paying off the mortgage, the sacrifice would be well worth it when you finish paying off the mortgage.

I recommend that you make paying off your mortgage early a part of your FINANCIAL PHILOSOPHY.

Idea Eight

TEACH YOUR KIDS ABOUT MONEY

It is important to teach your children about managing their money in a responsible way. Unfortunately, it is a skill that is not taught in schools or most homes so children are left on their own to figure this out later in life. Learning about money and how to manage it should be something that every child learns. This is not a skill that you want to learn by trial and error.

One method people use to teach children about money is called the "Bucket Method". There are two versions, the "Three Bucket" and the "Four Bucket" methods.

With the "Three Bucket" method, there are three separate buckets labeled, "SPENDING, SAVING and GIVING". When the child gets some money (allowance, gift, wages, etc.), it is divided up equally among the three buckets.

- One third goes into the SPENDING bucket and is used for anything she wants. She can spend it for whatever she wants to buy with no restrictions.

- One third goes into the SAVING bucket and is used to invest in long-term, income producing assets. This could be a CD or mutual fund or real estate depending on the age and financial sophistication of the child. This money should never be withdrawn for any reason.

- One third goes into the GIVING bucket and is to be given away to some worthy cause. This could be a church or charity that she likes or it could go to a neighbor who is in trouble financially.

Let's say that your son wants to make a major purchase. This is where the "Four Bucket" method is used. Let's say he wants to purchase a car. The fourth bucket would be labeled CAR. When the child gets some money (allowance, gift, wages, etc.), it is divided up equally among the four buckets.

- One quarter goes into the SPENDING bucket and is used for anything he wants. He can spend it for whatever he wants to buy with no restrictions.

- One quarter goes into the SAVING bucket and is used to invest in long-term, income producing assets. This could be a CD or mutual fund or real estate depending on the age and financial sophistication of the child. This money should never be withdrawn for any reason.

- One quarter goes into the GIVING bucket and is to be given away to some worthy cause. This could be a church or charity that he likes or it could go to a neighbor who is in trouble financially.

- One quarter goes into the CAR bucket and is left to accumulate until there is enough to purchase the car. The car should be purchased for the cash in the car bucket. It should never be used as a down payment on a car.

If you teach your children how to manage money, you will receive two benefits:

- You will learn how to manage money better

- Your children will become financially independent sooner in life. This takes the burden off you. Never allow your children to be financially dependent upon you after the age of 20.

I recommend that you make teaching your kids about money a part of your FINANCIAL PHILOSOPHY.

Idea Nine

LOTTERY WINNINGS AND INHERITANCES

*When it comes to money,
"Easy Come, Easy GO"
Is too often the truth!*

Inherited money, money given to you or money won in a lottery seems like a dream that many people would love to have in their lives. However, there are many studies that indicate that this windfall either ruins the lives of the recipients or results in them losing the whole thing within five short years. Strange as it may seem, bankruptcy often follows behind a large windfall. Instead of a dream, this often turns into a nightmare.

INHERITED MONEY

There are many stories of children of wealthy parents inheriting a fortune and spending it in one generation. One generation saw the parents work hard, sacrifice, save and invest and end up being wealthy. Then, unfortunately they don't pass on these values to their children. This is a huge mistake. When the children inherit control of the fortune without the values that created it, they don't know how to manage it properly. Often the result is that the children end up spending or losing the fortune in their lifetime.

> **THE PARENT'S GENERATION MAKES A FORTUNE**
> **THE CHILDREN'S GENERATION SQUANDERS THE FORTUNE**

In 1924, Barbara Hutton's grandmother died, leaving Barbara the Woolworth fortune in a trust fund. By the time of her 21st birthday in 1933, the value had increased to about $50 million (equivalent to $2.5 billion today).

> **FROM RAGS TO RICHES IN TWO GENERATIONS,**
> **FROM RICHES TO RAGS IN ONE GENERATION.**

But Barbara blew the Woolworth fortune in her lifetime. Can you imagine how difficult it would be to spend a few billion dollars? But through an extremely extravagant lifestyle and several bad choices of husbands, she managed to spend the whole fortune during her lifetime. Too often people in this situation don't have the values of being responsible or being a good steward of the money. Just think of the good that she could have done with that much money. She spent all that money during the Great Depression years when one third of the United States population was living in extreme poverty.

LOTTERY WINNINGS

Why would you buy a lottery ticket?

- It is fun?
- You could be rich?
- It is a wise investment?

Actually, the average lottery ticket buyer does it for all three. Lottery tickets as an investment may sound ludicrous to you but not to the type of person who buys them. Many people are hoping to acquire this tremendous windfall, but what they're really after is something that will make them happy?

Studies have shown that the typical buyer of lottery tickets is a lower income person who feels that they want to have a piece of the American dream but it is completely beyond their means. They feel that they could never earn or save enough to buy their own home. They feel hopeless. They are desperate to find a way to get ahead, to lead the good life. So, they buy a lottery ticket because it is the only way they see out of their hopeless state.

The lottery operators on average pay out in prizes only 62% of what they take in. The different states have pay out ranges from 20% to 80%. But since these are state run agencies, there is a certain percentage of the ticket money that is allocated to state projects. On average, this runs to over 35% of the income to the lottery ticket agency. By comparison, in Las Vegas the payout percentage for slot machines is usually over 90% of what is taken in. That is because there is competition in Las Vegas between casinos but there is no competition in a state with a lottery. Also in the Las Vegas casinos, there are no state projects to fund with the earnings.

Let's say that you are fortunate enough to be the big winner. It has been shown in study after study over the past fifty years that most lottery winners are worse off five years after winning the lottery than the day they bought the lottery ticket. Everyone says that it won't happen to them but statistics show that it probably will.

How could it go wrong? What happens if you win the lottery?

- it increases the odds that you will go bankrupt within 5 years
- it increases the likelihood of divorce
- it is such an upheaval in a person's life that it can lead to suicide
- it increases the likelihood that the winner or members of the family will have drug and alcohol problems
- it increases the number of people who want some of your money by whatever means they can use

- it can lead to paranoia
- it becomes the focus of your whole life

In the words of a lottery winner who won big,

"The key to staying happy is to hire a good financial planner and a good accountant. After paying off all debts, you should secure your future by making wise investments. Don't go on a crazy spending spree."

I recommend that you make managing lottery winnings and inheritances a part of your FINANCIAL PHILOSOPHY.

Idea Ten

BREAKING DOWN YOUR PAYCHECK

Once you have paid off all your consumer debts and saved your emergency fund, your paycheck is YOURS! Now when you get paid, you can decide how you want to allocate your paycheck in accordance with your goals and Life Plan.

What should you do with your paycheck at the end of the month? FINANCIAL FREEDOM means that you get to chose what you do with your money each month, not having your creditors tell you how you must spend your money.

Some people are so strapped that their entire paycheck goes to pay bills and minimum loan payments each month. Living like this is very stressful and expensive. There is always tension that arises from the balancing act of making minimum payments and keeping all your creditors satisfied. It is expensive because you are paying high interest rates and often fees such as late fees, over limit fees, overdraft fees, NSF fees and other fees and penalties which are very costly.

How do these people live? Often, by incurring more debt in the form of credit card debt!

USING YOUR CREDIT CARD IS INCURRING DEBT!

They are incurring debt without even knowing or thinking about it. Sometimes people act as if credit cards are free money. They can just spend and spend if the store will take their credit card. But unfortunately, they learn later that not only is it not free but that it has a huge price tag attached to it in the form of interest. Typically, credit card interest rates are between 18-24% per year. That equates to 1.5-2% per month which is more than most banks pay for a savings account for an entire year.

What is your FINANCIAL PHILOSOPHY regarding your paycheck? Here is what I suggest to you that could make a world of difference in your life. Break your paycheck into 4 parts each month and do things in the following order:

1. Give Away - 10% is given away to the church or charity of your choice

2. Saving - 10% goes into a savings account for major purchases

3. Saving - between 20% and 30% goes into a long-term investment account

4. Living Expenses - no more than 50% is what you live on each month

The percentages that you use are your choice. I would encourage you to devote more to item 3 Saving and less to item 4 Living Expenses. It may sound impossible but you can do it. Many people have been forced to do it by loss of income or pending bankruptcy if they didn't act. Once you adjust you will see that it is quite easy to live on half of your income.

While this may seem crazy, it works well if you practice it long term. Most of my working lifetime, I have followed an even more rigorous plan. I have given the first 10% to my church and charities that I believe in. I have saved between 40-60% of my income each month and invested it. I lived on the remaining 30-50%. If you develop a personal FINANCIAL PHILOSOPHY such as is taught in this book, then you too can live on less than 50% of your paycheck.

I recommend that you make breaking down your paycheck a part of your FINANCIAL PHILOSOPHY.

Idea Eleven

CONSIDER A ROTH IRA

A Roth IRA is a special retirement account that you fund with after-tax income. You don't get to deduct your contributions on your income tax return. Once you have made the contribution, all future withdrawals that follow Roth IRA regulations are tax free. This applies to what you put in and what was earned in the fund over the years.

There is no tax deduction for Roth IRA contributions as there is with a traditional IRA. This has kept a lot of people away from ROTH IRA's in the past. But I think that you should give them a second look. It depends on your age and your tax bracket—both now and in the future when you retire.

For people who are younger, the ROTH IRA is great because you have many years of future earnings that will not be taxed when you take the funds out later. If you are older, it makes less sense to use a ROTH IRA because you have a shorter time period between when you make your contributions and when you withdraw the funds in retirement.

Roth IRAs make the most sense if you expect your tax rate to be higher during retirement than your current rate. That makes Roth IRAs ideal savings vehicles for young, lower-income workers who won't miss the upfront tax deduction and will benefit from decades of tax-free, compounded growth. Roth IRAs also appeal to anyone who wants to minimize their tax bite in retirement, as well as older, wealthier taxpayers who want to leave assets to their heirs tax-free.

Unlike Traditional IRAs, you can take your money out of a Roth IRA tax free whenever you want. Some people don't understand how Traditional IRAs work. You don't pay any income tax on the money as it goes into an IRA account. However, you DO pay income tax on any money that you take out of an IRA.

A key difference between a traditional IRA and a ROTH IRA is what your current tax bracket is compared to what it will be later in retirement. Do you believe that tax rates are going to go up? Then the ROTH IRA may be better for you. Do you believe that the tax rates are going to go down? Then maybe the traditional IRA is best for you.

Given today's historically low federal tax rates and the large U.S. deficit, many economists believe federal income tax rates will rise in the future – meaning Roth IRAs may be the better long-term choice. But of course, no one knows.

Finally, when you have a traditional IRA you have deferred paying income tax on the funds. The IRS would like you to pay that tax, so starting at age 70 ½ you must start taking Required Minimum Distributions (RMD's) to pay out the full amount over your expected remaining life time. Of course, the RMD's are fully taxable so you will be losing a portion of this money to income taxes.

However, with ROTH IRA's you have already paid the income taxes so the money can stay inside the ROTH IRA and continue to earn money tax free for years. Also, if you are working, you can continue to contribute to a ROTH IRA unlike a traditional IRA.

An extra bonus is that you can give 100% of your ROTH IRA to your beneficiary when you die and it is TAX FREE to him. The beneficiary must withdraw the money from the ROTH IRA during his lifetime but it is all tax free.

I recommend that you make investing in a Roth IRA a part of your FINANCIAL PHILOSOPHY.

Appendix A

BRUCE'S FINANCIAL PHILOSOPHY

Here is my personal FINANCIAL PHILOSOPHY:

- spend less than I earn every month
- work at a second job
- save at least 50% of my main salary
- avoid all consumer debt
- avoid car loans
- avoid student loans
- invest in income producing assets
- give generously to church and charity
- always pay my credit card bill in full every month
- do not use debit cards
- save up and pay cash for large purchases
- never pay more than $5,000 for a vehicle
- buy a modest home

- purchase real estate for investment
- incur a mortgage only if necessary
- pay off any mortgage ASAP
- work in retirement but not to make money
- spend money on experiences and not things
- keep $10,000 in an emergency fund available for use
- take advantage of tax deferred programs
- cash flow is more important than equity
- insurance is not necessary for me

ABOUT THE AUTHOR

Bruce Raine is an Income Tax Accountant who uses his wealth of accounting experience to specialize in working with real estate investors, small businesses and self-employed individuals. He is also a public speaker and the author of Attitude Determines Destiny, Attitude Determines Your Destiny and Income Tax Issues for Small Businesses and Self-Employed Individuals.

His experience working at Deloitte as an auditor and teaching at California State University in Hayward give him a broad perspective on financial matters. Bruce has been a public speaker in both Canada and the United States.

Bruce is available to assist you in the following services:

- Income Tax Return preparation

- Seminars and Workshops on Income Taxes

- Seminars and Workshops on Achieving Financial Freedom

- Dealing with issues that arise with the IRS or FTB
- Evaluating your tax return to ensure you took advantage of all possible deductions

You can contact Bruce at
www.BruceRaineTaxes.com
or 925-336-4518 or at

111 Deerwood Road, Suite 200
San Ramon, CA 94583.

COACHING

Bruce Raine has a personal conviction that people living in the United States of America should be financially free. It is possible to become very rich in the United States. However, that is not what this book is about. It is about achieving FINANIAL FREEDOM which means that you can do what you want when you retire – or maybe even sooner.

Bruce is available to coach individuals and couples who need advice and guidance with their personal finances. Bruce charges a small annual fee to help people get out of debt and on their way to preparing for retirement.

You can contact Bruce at
www.BruceRaineTaxes.com or
925-336-4518 or at

111 Deerwood Road, Suite 200
San Ramon, CA 94583.

100% MONEY BACK GUARANTEE!

I GUARANTEE that this book is worth the purchase price or I will give you your money back – 100% of your purchase price.

If you read this book, applied the advice given and feel that it is not worth the price that you paid, I will give you your money back.

It is extremely important to me that you are satisfied with the book. If you would like to send me a letter telling about how you liked or disliked the book, I would truly appreciate it. If you see how this book can be improved, please send in your suggestions.

However, if you are so dissatisfied that you want your money back, just complete the steps below:

Send me a letter verifying that you read the whole book.

Send me a letter explaining why you are dissatisfied. I would like to know how you feel this book let you down.

Return the book regardless of the condition.

Send me a copy of the receipt showing the date and amount of the purchase.

You can contact Bruce at
www.BruceRaineTaxes.com or
925-336-4518 or at

111 Deerwood Road, Suite 200
San Ramon, CA 94583.

BOOK BRUCE RAINE TO SPEAK AT YOUR NEXT EVENT

Do you want your next meeting to be more meaningful for the attendees?

Do you want them going home saying, "This was the best meeting that I ever attended!"?

Then contact Bruce and ask about having him as a workshop presenter for your next meeting.

Since 1977 Bruce has been speaking to audiences in Canada and the United States about various subjects:

- motivation
- personal finances
- income tax issues for small business owners and self-employed individuals
- income tax issues for real estate investors
- history
- stories

Bruce has more than 10,000 hours speaking in front of groups. He will produce a custom message for your group that will inspire them to do greater things than they are doing now. Bruce has a treasure trove of stories both humorous and meaningful that will entertain your group. They will be learning even though they may not realize it.

> **THERE IS SELDOM A DULL MOMENT**
> **IN ONE OF BRUCE'S WORKSHOPS**

You can contact Bruce at
www.BruceRaineTaxes.com or
925-336-4518 or at

111 Deerwood Road, Suite 200
San Ramon, CA 94583.

Made in the USA
Columbia, SC
05 February 2019